Self Study Problems
for **CANADIAN FINANCIAL ACCOUNTING**

Self Study Problems

for **CANADIAN FINANCIAL ACCOUNTING**

G.D. Richardson / L.S. Rosen

Prentice-Hall of Canada, Ltd.
Scarborough, Ontario

Canadian Cataloguing in Publication Data

Richardson, Gordon D.
   Self study problems for Canadian financial
accounting

Supplement to: Rosen, Lawrence S., 1935-   Canadian
financial accounting.
ISBN 0-13-113167-2

1. Accounting - Canada - Problems, exercises, etc.
I. Rosen, Lawrence S., 1935-   II. Rosen, Lawrence
S., 1935-   Canadian financial accounting. III. Title.

HF5635.R683   657'.0971   C80-094741-X

Prentice-hall, Inc., Englewood Cliffs, New Jersey
Prentice-Hall of Australia, Pty., Ltd., Sydney
Prentice-Hall of India Pvt., Ltd., New Delhi
Prentice-Hall International, Inc., London
Prentice-Hall of Japan, Inc., Tokyo
Prentice-Hall of Southeast Asia (Pte.) Ltd., Singapore

Production Editor, Design: Beth Clelland
Artwork: Barbara Steel
Cover: Joe Chin

ISBN 0-13-113167-2

1 2 3 4 5 WC 84 83 82 81 80

Contents

Preface

WHAT TO EXPECT

Self Study Problems for Canadian Financial Accounting (SSP) is designed
to give students of introductory financial accounting, particularly those
using *Canadian Financial Accounting: Principles and Issues (CFA)*, extra
practice in problem solving. Important concepts have been built into
carefully selected problems which are provided in both *SSP* and *CFA*. *SSP*
comprises solutions to those problems from *CFA* marked with an asterisk;
many new problems and a few examples for students to work out, all with
accompanying possible solutions; and further discussion of some textbook
topics. The approximate time it takes to work out problems is indicated
in parentheses following problem numbers. Students can do the problems
on their own time, and correct them at their convenience by looking at
the full explanations and solutions. If any unanswered questions remain
after a study of the responses in *SSP*, then students are advised to ask
their instructor or a grader of their assignments. For the most part,
SSP is designed, as its title indicates, for self study, and it should
answer most of your concerns about problem solving and major concepts.

A typical financial accounting[1] course builds from class to class. Consequently, it is wise to study the material each week, especially until
Chapter 5 has been completed. A poor understanding of Chapter 3, for
example, will have a major effect on your grasp of Chapter 4. Avoid
getting behind: education experiments in accounting indicate that those
who study in advance of discussions in the classroom do much better on
examinations.

In the authors' experiences, introductory accounting students often feel
insecure about their understanding of the subject. Many times this feeling is a result of expecting "too much" from one course. Accounting

_____

[1]Meaning accounting designed in large measure for those persons outside
of the company, such as shareholders, creditors, and Revenue Canada.

deals with a changing world which is full of uncertainties. Do not expect accounting to be precise or to be a haven from this uncertain world. There are few absolute "rights" or "wrongs" in accounting. If you search for "truths," you will become frustrated. As you move through the course, your uncomfortable feeling might very well grow. If possible, avoid venting your insecurities and frustrations on the subject, and on your instructors, graders and tutorial leaders. The latter individuals need your support in trying to communicate difficult themes.

DESIGN OF CFA

Chapters 1 and 2 of *CFA* provide a large number of new terms; you are certainly not expected to remember most of these by the time you finish reading Chapter 2. New terms will be repeated from place to place in either or both *CFA* and *SSP*. Chapter 2 in particular is an overview of the book, and may overwhelm you: that is not its purpose. Chapter 2 is designed to tell you where we are headed and to let you see a larger picture of the whole subject before we go into depth in some topics.

A good grasp of Chapters 3 and 4 is essential to comprehension of many parts of succeeding chapters. You should try to get into the themes of Chapters 3 and 4 as soon as you can—if possible, in advance of coverage by an instructor, or as indicated in a correspondence course. When you feel comfortable with Chapter 4, read the Appendices to it.

Chapter 5 may seem to be a contrast to the rules in Chapters 3 and 4. Chapter 5 lets you know that the subject is far more complex than you might have thought before registering for the course. It is *important* at this point in your studies to develop a sensible *attitude*. Try to view your role as one of ascertaining the circumstances where a specific accounting method or policy *makes sense*, and where it does *not* make sense. Avoid searching for the one, all-purpose answer, or "truth." Memorization of "rules" may have been helpful in studying Chapters 3 and 4, but it can prove troublesome if used extensively in learning the variations in Chapter 5.

Chapters 6 through 12 repeat the themes of the first five chapters, using specific assets and liabilities as examples. In studying these seven chapters try to identify the themes as being repeats of what you have seen before. Most themes are not new, but they may be variations of concepts noted in Chapter 5.

Chapters 13 through 16 are of a more specialized nature, and some or all may not be assigned in your course. Chapter 13 is complex. It is one of those subjects that causes problems for authors of textbooks: a little knowledge can be misleading, but reasonable coverage can be beyond intro-ductory students. We have chosen to give a realistic picture of the subject and therefore have risked confusing you. However, we have found that after a careful second or third reading by students, the material can be assimilated.

Chapter 14 will indicate to you how well you have retained the detailed concepts in Chapters 3 and 4 and the broad ideas in the other chapters. The material is an excellent integrating and review device for instructors, and tends to be a favourite for examinations because it tests several topics.

Chapter 15 focuses more directly than other chapters upon users of financial statements, especially bankers and analysts who act on behalf of prospective long-term creditors and shareholders. Even if the chapter is not assigned in your course, you will probably find it interesting even after you have completed the course.

Chapter 16 is directed at the future measurement systems of accounting. The capital maintenance philosophies noted in this chapter will receive greater attention in the next decade. Those who proceed with subsequent accounting courses ought to find Chapters 13 through 16 useful references.

WHAT TO LOOK FOR

Financial accounting reports and statements are the result of compromises between preparers and users. The course must therefore cover both viewpoints on all issues which we encounter.

Our approach may be different from that taken by some of your friends in other institutions or programs, or in high schools. For example, they may have spent most of their time on a preparer viewpoint, and been told why and how accountants have rationalized their "traditions." We do not believe that such a course explains accounting as it currently exists nor the direction in which it appears to be heading. Such a course may also concentrate too much on knowledge -- including knowledge which will soon become obsolete -- and devote insufficient time to other analytical and judgment skills.

Our approach is more challenging than some of the conventional introductory financial accounting courses which have been offered in Canada. Yet, we know from having class-tested the material that most students can handle it and are well satisfied with the results.

Let us now try to describe one possible environment of learning financial accounting which we would like you to keep in mind as you study the subject. Our sketch is not intended as the only possible description of an accounting learning environment. It is provided so that you can better grasp why we are exposing you to particular themes or "commercials." We are not really asking you to run before you can crawl. We do, however, go to some pains to make sure that the way you learn to crawl can make the transition to walking and running easier. We want to avoid giving you the impression that bookkeeping is the same as accounting. They are quite different. Bookkeepers can avoid making judgments and having to tailor accounting to its environment. We do not want some of you attracted to a career that is unsuited to you. Finally, we do not want to "turn off" those who might become successful financial executives and auditors.

x

There are five main parties involved in the learning of financial accounting:

1. Students:
   - Want to be eased into the subject by being provided with fundamental building blocks which will last forever.
   - A few want time-tested, polished techniques such as may exist on successful television programs. They are not in favour of trial and error learning, and understanding which comes from making mistakes.
   - Many want to avoid developing a false sense of security and false direction for future courses.
   - Many want one course to provide them with the abilities to read financial statements and to avoid making mistakes.

2. Instructors:
   - Want students to develop a broad understanding of the subject and to build comprehensive foundations, to which they can attach their future experiences and thereby expand their understanding.
   - Want to teach what is best taught at a university and to avoid teaching material which is best taught on-the-job, or likely to become obsolete quickly.
   - Want students to avoid memorization of material which is not really "fact" but varies with circumstances.
   - Want students to develop analytical processes, especially the ability to reason from problem identification through data analysis to logical, supported recommendations.

3. Preparers of financial statements:
   - Have to be concerned with a variety of objectives, facts, and constraints, and know how to tailor accounting techniques and report to the specific situation. Judgment must be developed.
   - Have to pay attention to cost-benefit relationships and not prepare financial statements which are inappropriate.
   - Have to be aware of legal liability and how a preparer might be sued for issuing misleading financial statements which cause users to suffer financial losses.

4. Users of financial statements:
   - Hope to be able to use the financial statements to make a variety of judgments.
   - Seek comparability among companies in financial reporting but know this may be difficult for preparers to attain.
   - May not want to pay for financial information, but expect to have it freely available, like air.
   - Are justifiably critical of some accounting techniques which cloud financial results. (These techniques are mentioned from place to place in the textbook.)

5. Auditors of financial statements:
   - Are required by law to attest to the fairness of financial statements in accordance with generally accepted accounting principles (GAAP). They do *not* attest to fairness as such because "fairness"

is a difficult concept to define operationally. They attest to
"fairness per GAAP."
- They do not choose accounting principles for a client. All they
  are required to do is attest that the client has selected one of a
  group of acceptable principles or practices per GAAP.
- They can be sued by a user for attesting to financial statements
  which are misleading and cause the user to suffer financial losses.
- They have to exercise judgment in financial accounting and reporting.

This description will not mean much to you at an early point in the course.
What we are trying to convey is that the environment of accounting is
broad. The five parties of the environment must interact with each other,
even though they have different interests and concerns. The sooner we can
move towards understanding a broader picture of the subject, the better
off we will be.

Back to our "commercial." If students put pressure on instructors to give
too many problems which have one "correct" answer, they are working
against their own education. The five-part scenario we have just described is *not* one of certainty of outcomes or results. Although journal
entries are a part of the accounting process, they are not an end in themselves. The *end* is better judgments. Students have to learn how to
evaluate and *apply* accounting in a judgment or decision setting.

Students will receive the type of education that they demand. Instructors
can be intimidated by student demands for simplicity and security.

We urge you to read those sections of the textbook which describe the
environment of accounting. Such a reading is needed to counterbalance the
heavy emphasis on problem solving in this book.

Acknowledgments

Canadian Financial Accounting: Principles and Issues lists the names of several organizations and individuals who provided help during its preparation. We would like to express our appreciation to them once more.

In preparing this student aid, we received assistance from Joe Bolla of Price Waterhouse & Co. and from our industrious secretaries, Lillian Leonard and Denise Timmons. We are grateful to them.

Comments from students are welcome.

G. D. Richardson
L. S. Rosen

Toronto, Canada.

Introduction

OVERVIEW

The remarks in *this* chapter will be difficult for you to understand at
this point in the course. However, we must include them somewhere in
order to give you a larger picture of the subject: the beginning of the
course is as good a place as any. In approaching this material it is
vital that you:

1. Avoid thinking that the course is going to be too difficult for you.
    After you have studied the first five chapters of the textbook, the
    material in this chapter will be making considerable sense to you.
    You will be able to use this chapter to build a model for understand-
    ing the subject of financial accounting.

2. Make a commitment to yourself to read what is in this chapter at
    several places in the course. Frequent reference will help to keep
    you on track for where we are headed. On each reading, you will
    understand more, and you will be able to see why accountants handle
    situations the way they do and why readers of the financial statements
    may or may not be pleased.

3. Keep an open mind concerning the educational "commercials" that we
    occasionally provide. The pressures are great to turn an introductory
    accounting course into bookkeeping lessons. We must avoid leaving you
    with a bookkeeper's outlook.

EDUCATIONAL OBJECTIVES

When students and educators are aware of the objectives or purposes of
education in general terms and how these objectives are being pursued in
a particular course, the reasons for learning become more apparent and
learning itself perhaps becomes easier. Various classifications of
educational objectives exist; one which makes sense for university level

accounting courses contains six categories of skills[1]: 1) knowledge, 2) comprehension, 3) application, 4) analysis, 5) synthesis, and 6) evaluation.

Knowledge is usually defined as the ability to remember or recall. Comprehension is the ability to understand what is being communicated. Application is the ability to use knowledge in concrete situations. Analysis is the ability to identify significant relationships, distinguish fact from guesses or hypotheses, and subdivide a problem into its parts. Synthesis is the ability to combine learning skills, tools and techniques into an understandable model. Evaluation is the ability to make judgments and offer recommendations.

Accounting courses that are offered in high schools and some junior colleges tend to focus primarily on knowledge, secondarily (but often a distant second) on comprehension, and thirdly (if at all) on the other four skills. There is nothing wrong with focusing primarily or exclusively on knowledge (and memorization), as long as you aspire to be a bookkeeper employed by an accountant who is available to handle the other skills. But those who aspire to managerial and senior accounting positions must acquire all six skills.

The challenge for university-level educators, a major concern, is to introduce the five skills, in addition to knowledge, at suitable times, so that students progress but avoid excessive frustration. The textbook, *Canadian Financial Accounting: Principles and Issues*, tries to provide flexibility for instructors so that they can tailor their course to the desires and needs of the students. There are many sections in the textbook, and many questions and problems, which are designed to convey and test knowledge. Other portions are designed for the other five skills. Some instructors may want to assign only those items concerned with knowledge. Other instructors may want to pull you through the other five skills. When they do, the frustration level of the class increases. So far, educators have not found a painless way of conveying analysis, evaluation and similar skills.

Instructors especially need your cooperation when they are exposing you to application, analysis, synthesis, and evaluation. A dialogue among class members and the instructor is essential, so that feedback is quick and corrective action is timely.

Students tend to receive the type of education which they request. If the class demands a concentration on knowledge (through seeking lectures with little class participation or give-and-take, and examinations that mainly test memorization and narrow interpretations), then it must accept the consequences. One consequence is that students may have to learn the other

---

[1]See Benjamin S. Bloom, ed. *Taxonomy of Educational Objectives, Handbook I: Cognitive Domain* (Longmans, Green & Co., 1956); and E. B. Deakin III, M. H. Granof and C. H. Smith, "Educational Objectives for an Accounting Program", *The Accounting Review* (July 1974), pp.584-589.

skills in later courses or when they graduate. That is not easy.
Employers often seek more than a knowledge skill, especially in accounting, since knowledge is dated and can quickly become obsolete.

We cannot overemphasize the dangers of a strict focus on knowledge.
Students often do not realize that their actions (such as not reading in
advance of class meetings, or excessive complaining about examinations
which require throught) tend to pressure instructors into teaching only
knowledge.

ENVIRONMENT

Chapters 1 and 2 are devoted to the environment or place of financial
accounting. Financial accounting can be contrasted with management
accounting, which involves recording and reporting to management. Financial accounting can be used by the managers of an organization, but it is
mainly designed for those outside of the enterprise. The "outsiders"
have different desires -- a matter which is explored in Question 1-1 of
the textbook.

This understanding of the environment is a necessary antidote to the heavy
exposure to the bookkeeping cycle that is discussed in Chapters 3 to 5.
In Chapters 3 to 5 and some sections of subsequent chapters, we give prime
attention to current knowledge. We ignore different users and uses,
simplify facts, and make many assumptions which reduce the complexity and
reality of a situation. For the most part we adopt the viewpoint of a
preparer--not a typical preparer we must hastily add--who thinks that
there is one, correct way of accounting for and reporting each transaction.

When we are learning a new subject, we have to start with simple issues
and build upon them. However, it can be a very serious mistake to assume
that these simple issues are basics, or foundations upon which everything
else can be built. Accounting "basics" comprise the six skills noted
earlier plus many others, such as the ability to communicate orally and in
writing. It is wise to start disciplining yourself now so that you avoid
locking into Chapters 3 and 4, and thinking that they alone are the basic
building blocks of the course and the subject of accountancy.

TEXTBOOK *1-1: A RESPONSE (30-60 minutes)

The response which follows likely will seem overwhelming at this point in
the course, but the points will become clearer as we proceed. Chapter 5
especially will help iι fitting the pieces together. We are providing a
lengthy response at this stage because we want you to know where we are
headed. We do not expect you to memorize the points noted. Rather, we
wish to paint a broad picture of the preparer-user viewpoint of financial
accounting so that you avoid seeking simple answers to complex issues.
Several points are in abbreviated form; they will be expanded later.
Focus on the general theme which emerges. Try to read the response provided here after you read every one or two chapters of the textbook.

a. The U.S. Financial Accounting Standards Board Statement of Financial

Concepts No.1 on *Objectives of Financial Reporting by Business
Enterprises* contains a rather useful list of potential users, as
follows:

Many people base economic decisions on their relationships
to and knowledge about business enterprises and thus are
potentially interested in the information provided by financial reporting. Among the potential users are owners,
lenders, suppliers, potential investors and creditors,
employees, management, directors, customers, financial analysts and advisors, brokers, underwriters, stock exchanges,
lawyers, economists, taxing authorities, regulatory
authorities, legislators, financial press and reporting
agencies, labour unions, trade associations, business
researchers, teachers and students, and the public. Members
and potential members of some groups -- such as owners,
creditors, and employees -- have or contemplate having direct
economic interests in particular business enterprises.
Managers and directors, who are charged with managing the
enterprise in the interest of owners, also have a direct
interest. Members of other groups -- such as financial analysts and advisors, regulatory authorities, and labour
unions -- have direct or indirect interests because they
advise or represent those who have or contemplate having
direct interests.[2]

It should be noted that there are many diverse users of financial
statements. A major theme of this text is that the needs of no one
group are paramount in all situations. In one instance, it may be
the needs of management (who are preparers of statements) that are
most important (perhaps with respect to performance appraisal). In
another, the needs of creditors may be most important, and careful
disclosure related to cash flow (receipts less disbursements) may be
critical. In yet another instance, the needs of investors who trade
shares might be most important, thus making earnings measurement and
trends (for cash flow prediction) important. In still another case,
shares might not be traded publicly and stewardship might be the
dominant concern of present shareholders. Accounting information
should be tailored to suit the objectives of the preparer and important
users at hand, as well as the facts and constraints present.

b. The decisions facing the preparer and various users include:

Shareholders - buying, selling, or holding shares in a limited com-
                 pany (hence, prediction of cash flows becomes
                 important).
               - the remuneration (salary) and promotion or discon-
                 tinuance of present management (hence, performance
                 appraisal).

---

[2]FASB, Statement of Financial Accounting Concepts No.1, *Objectives of
Financial Reporting by Business Enterprises* (Stamford: FASB, 1978).

	- the assessment of management's custody over assets entrusted to it (hence, stewardship).
Management	- the measurement of income taxes payable (sometimes related to accounting earnings). - how to portray its own performance (for bonus purposes, etc.). - internal control over assets entrusted to it (through double entry bookkeeping).
Creditors	- decision as to amounts they are willing to lend, the interest rate, terms of repayment, any loan provisions or restrictions (hence, prediction of future cash flows becomes important). - evaluation of management's ability. - decision as to the ability of the borrower to repay the loan, perhaps in short term (hence, portrayal of short term cash position or liquidity may be important; this is distinct from long run prediction of future earnings). - decision as to the value of any underlying security (usually inventories or receivables; this is related to the prediction objective).
Government agencies	- monitor compliance with a statute such as the Canada Business Corporations Act. - assess income tax payable (i.e., Department of National Revenue). - anti-combines investigations (conspiracy to fix prices).
Securities commissions	- monitor compliance with securities legislation.
Financial analysts	- similar to the needs of investors outlined above.
Credit rating agencies	- similar to the needs of creditors outlined above.
Suppliers	- decision to extend credit; similar to creditors.
Customers	- the decision to accept the company as a supplier may require a look at the financial strength of the company; therefore, the situation is similar to both investors and creditors.
Employees, unions	- collective bargaining decisions. - decision to accept a senior position in the company.
Competitors	- strategic decisions within a given market segment.

c. The information needs of the above preparers or users follow from
   their decisions, as outlined above.

User	Decision	Information needs
Shareholders, Creditors	Investment or loan decisions	*Predict* future cash flows (receipts and disbursements) and assess any uncertainty (risk) associated with those flows. The following can, if carefully designed, facilitate the prediction objective (These are explained later in the textbook): - departmental or segmented data, not just the totals for an entire company. - quarterly reports, instead of just annual ones. - current value measures, not just original costs. - unusual, extraordinary item treatment of some financial transactions. - footnote disclosure of additional information not easily measured on the financial statements.
	Remuneration, hire/fire/promote decision	*Performance appraisal* information. Shareholders need to know which aspects of company's performance were beyond management's control (windfalls or lucky consequences, etc.) and which were not. Careful disclosure on the statements and in the notes may facilitate this.
	Assess management's custody (fraud prevention and detection, etc.)	*Stewardship* information about what management did with assets entrusted to it. Most accounting data are pertinent to this objective.
Management	Measure income taxes payable	Management needs to know how the selection of an accounting policy (i.e., when to increase a company's worth) could affect income taxes payable. Possibly less expensive alternatives

- 6 -

User	Decision	Information needs
		could be selected.
	Portray its own performance	See above re shareholders. Management often wants to present earnings trends in a favourable light. (We will have more to say about this later in the textbook.)
Creditors	Loan decision	Prediction – see above. *Liquidity* assessment. This is very close to prediction but is more immediate in nature. Creditors (especially if short-term) need to know what liquid assets such as cash are presently available to meet current claims or debts. Collateral or assets pledged to the creditor in case the loan is not repaid. The current worth of assets is important to some creditors.
Government agencies		Specific disclosure requirements are contained in corporate legislation. General needs of other users may be specified in various laws (statutes).
Securities commissions		Specific disclosure requirements are noted in legislation. Sufficient disclosure in general is required to keep the "prudent investor" informed (calls for judgment in each circumstance).
Financial analysts / credit rating agencies		Similar to investors and creditors but information usually is needed in more depth; occasionally analysts will directly ask the company for information (forecasts, etc.). Generally, analysts want a great deal of disclosure because they do not have to pay the costs of assembling it.
Suppliers/ customers		Similar to investors and creditors.

Users	Decision	Information needs
Employees, unions		Similar to investors and creditors.
Competitors		Any strategically-useful information is sought; but the preparer may want to avoid giving information to shareholders if it will prove helpful to competitors.

d. As indicated in the text, "it is virtually impossible to prepare a general purpose report which satisfactorily serves the needs of all potential users." The sheer amount of disclosure required explains the "impossibility." Hence, tradeoffs must be made; priorities must be established. This is one important source of potential conflict between users - the competition for *more* information for their particular purpose. Another source of conflict arises when disclosure would benefit some groups (say potential investors or lenders; competitors) but is resisted by other groups (say present management and shareholders), perhaps due to the cost of disclosure, or for other reasons. Some common conflicts include:

i. Income tax versus other user needs - statements might be prepared *primarily* for income tax purposes and resulting financial statements might be less useful for other purposes (i.e. earnings or cash flow prediction). An example is conservative revenue recognition policies, which is explained in Chapter 5.

ii. Stewardship versus prediction - the stewardship objective is best satisfied by "objective" information. The prediction objective is best satisfied by "relevant" information, including "soft" information like cash flow forecasts, market value estimates, etc. This is the familiar tradeoff between objectivity and relevance.

iii. Competitors versus the company - competitors often look to financial statements of their competitors to glean any information useful for strategic purposes. Hence, companies tend to resist demands for increased disclosure of the profitability of individual products or other segment data.

iv. Internal uses (say, a bonus to managers) versus external uses - often a bonus formula is linked to earnings and, if not designed carefully, may motivate management to "manage" or smooth the earnings picture accordingly. The entire "income smoothing" controversy relates to management's desire, given a choice between accounting principles, to select principles which portray a desired earnings trend.

v. Accrual accounting versus cash flows - sometimes the employment of accrual accounting and matching (for stewardship) results in values and earnings measures which bear little resemblance to

available *cash*, thus hindering prediction of cash flows.
Examples are the inclusion in inventory of items which are
almost obsolete or slow moving; and wealth recognition in advance
of the receipt of cash, where cash collection is not assured, or
estimable. (These points are discussed further in Chapter 5.)

e. Where conflicts exist, the accountant must establish priorities
between objectives, after considering the various objectives, facts
and constraints at hand in each particular instance. For example, a
public company reporting to provincial securities commissions must
often keep the needs of investors and long term creditors uppermost
in mind (hence, prediction and stewardship are uppermost). Performance appraisal and income tax become secondary considerations. On
the other hand, a small closely-held company with no debt might make
the income tax minimization objective first priority; stewardship and
prediction become less important; bonus formulas for owner-managers
may become an important consideration. The same small company with
a bank loan payable on demand must keep the needs of the bank in mind.
The banker is likely very interested in the measurement of receivables
and inventories but less interested, say, in the choice of depreciation policies. The textbook provides many different examples of this
kind, reinforcing the need to tailor accounting recommendations to
specific objectives/facts/constraints.

TEXTBOOK *1-7: A SOLUTION (60-90 minutes)

a. The purpose of this question is to encourage the student to start to
develop a logical approach which can be used to solve more complex
accounting problems and cases. One such approach is to ask oneself:
For whom (which users) and for what purposes are accounting reports
and statements (e.g., as for Home Heating Oil) being prepared? Are
they requested by a bank's loan officer? If so, information on short-
term asset liquidity may be needed. Are the statements being
requested by a long-term creditor? If so, information on compliance
with legal restrictions may be a critical need. Perhaps there are no
creditors and only one shareholder, so that the statements are being
prepared mainly for income tax filing purposes (hence, income tax
related considerations may be critical). Or, perhaps there are all
of the above uses (and users) but in addition the statements are used
by owners of a public company (shareholders) and security analysts,
in which case measurement of income or earnings (hence, trends which
help predict future income growth prospects and future cash flows)
may be of great importance.

Once critical information requirements are identified, accounting
measurement of revenue and expenses and accompanying explanations or
disclosure can be tailored accordingly, particularly where choice
exists. This text contains many examples of where such choice exists
for the accountant. A few such examples are:

- whether to expense on the income statement certain costs which are
  "capital" in nature (say, costs of developing a new product) or

recognize them as an asset, as per the "matching" principle (to be explained in Chapter 5).
- the choice of timing of revenue recognition on an income statement (after completion of production, after shipment, after receipt of cash, and so on, as explained in Chapter 5).
- when to recognize a permanent loss in value or impairment of an asset (hence, when to write the asset "down" on the balance sheet).
- how much to disclose in notes to financial statements when describing an event or transaction.

The student must recognize that before any accounting treatment can be selected from the many competing alternatives, specific user needs and information requirements *must* be identified (as well as relevant facts and legislative and other constraints, as explained in later chapters --Chapter 1 focuses mainly on user needs).

At this point in the course, instructors do not expect you to understand all of the above matters. But they want you to start looking for these thoughts as you read and study. This question and its "solution" should be referred to once per week as the course progresses.

In this question, the four users are identified for the student. This makes the job easier. For many other problems and cases in this text, it will be left to the student to identify which users are likely to exist in a particular situation and how accounting might be used to satisfy their particular information requirements.

The information requirements of our four users include the following:

Loan officer

The loan officer is interested in security or protection for the loan and in short-term liquidity, in order to decide whether to issue a loan or perhaps to request repayment of a loan outstanding. That is, the officer is interested in the amount of cash which can be generated by assets in the short term to meet imminent cash obligations (including the obligation to the bank to repay the loan. This bank loan often takes priority over other creditors for repayment because the loan is secured, usually by receivables and inventories).

The measurement of short term assets (accounts receivable, inventory) and short term liabilities (accrued liabilities, currently-due long term debt) is of interest to the loan officer, since resulting working capital ratios (excess of current assets over current liabilities, to be discussed later in the textbook) often play an important part in the loan decision. Some loan officers have to follow rules given to them by head office. These rules stipulate what working capital and other financial statement ratios have to be before a loan can be granted.

DNR (Department of National Revenue re income taxation)

The DNR wants to assess whether the company has measured income for income tax purposes as specified by the Income Tax Act. Sometimes the figure for DNR will differ from accounting income due to expenses or revenues which are not allowed (say, accounting depreciation or certain loss provisions) by the Income Tax Act. Equally important, sometimes a wide variety of accounting treatment (say, recording revenue on the income statement) will be accepted by tax authorities for tax purposes, so that all of the DNR, other users and the preparer are interested in which *one* of the accounting policies and methods of recording is chosen.

Shareholder (Owners of one type of company are called common shareholders)

The shareholder wants to predict future dividends and capital gains (increases in share value) in order to decide whether to buy, sell, or hold a common share (the prediction objective). In order to predict, the shareholder typically wants information on earnings and income statement trends. Earnings or income measurement (which involves subtracting expenses from revenues) becomes critical. This expense-recording process requires the allocations of long term asset costs to each time period. An example is depreciation and is something which a creditor or the DNR may be less interested in.

The shareholder also wants to assess management's stewardship over assets entrusted (detection of fraud, etc.) and to assess management's performance (perhaps a bonus to managers is based on recorded income). Financial statements are often referred to for this purpose, particularly since they are often attested to or checked by auditors.

Long term creditor

May be similar in viewpoint to that of a bank loan officer except:
- security for the loan is often more fixed in nature. For example, the plant building may be mortgaged. Hence, information is desired on the current value or worth of such long term plant assets, which may have to be sold to pay off a long term loan.
- the creditor is not able to call for repayment of the loan at will, protections (called covenants) and other restrictions are often written into the loan contract. The accountant must disclose if these covenants and restrictions have been violated by management.
- the creditor lends for the longer term and is likely more interested in the long term cash flow picture than the loan officer is. Hence, prediction and revenue and expense trends may be of some importance to the long term creditor.

b. Accounting is only one source of information. Other information may be more important for:

Shareholders	– discussions with management – earnings forecasts of management – stockbroker or financial analyst – industry reports, magazines, etc. – information filed with securities commission
Creditors (short and long term)	– credit reports – information filed with securities commission (if sale to public) – bond rating services – professional appraisals of assets – discussions with management
Department of National Revenue	– specific forms filled out for income tax purposes – investigations of company – discussions with management

The student should be aware of some of the implications of the existence of diverse user groups and their information sources:

– Each of the four users referred to (and there are many other users not referred to) have different information requirements, with some overlap, as discussed in 1-7a. above.

– One set of general purpose financial statements will often not satisfy all of the financial information needs of all of these users. The financial statements, by themselves, are not likely to be sufficient as the sole source for making decisions, for any of the users identified above.

– An important point for students to keep in mind is that some user groups (creditors, the DNR) have the power to force the company to issue special purpose reports tailored to their needs. The shareholder is often not in the same position and hence is protected by company legislation and securities commissions, which place important constraints on companies and require minimum information for shareholders.

When asked to resolve a financial reporting problem (choice of journal entries, choice of disclosure, etc., all of which are discussed later), the student might benefit from a logic process such as the following:

1. Who are the likely users of financial statements in this situation?

2. What are their information requirements?

3. How can a choice of accounting measurement or disclosure help satisfy these requirements?

4. Does conflict exist regarding the choice in 3. above? Would the selection of one method of recording (for example, a method which recognizes revenue at the completion of production) satisfy one user's requirements (the need of shareholders to predict future cash inflows to the company) yet hinder other users' requirements (say, the need of creditors to assess the extent to which the receivable can be converted to instant cash; or, the need of the company to postpone the recognition of revenue for income tax purposes as long as possible)?

5. If conflict does exist, and if only a few users' needs can be catered to, can users be ranked in order of their importance? This requires judgment by the student. The needs of shareholders are important because financial statements (discussed in greater depth in Chapter 2) are prepared first and foremost for shareholders. However, the needs of "third parties" such as creditors and the DNR are obviously important also. A company may need a bank loan in order to survive.

6. Once any conflict is resolved, the student is in a position to select, say, a journal entry (discussed in Chapter 3) which best suits the most relevant user needs at hand. In the example cited in 4., perhaps the prediction needs of shareholders are paramount. Hence, earlier revenue recognition may be justified. (Chapter 5 expands on this point.)

7. While it may seem conjectural to consider what additional sources of information are available to specific users, the student may want to consider these as some support for a selected method of recording or disclosure. For example, in the situation described in 4., the student may decide that, in a particular situation, the short or long-term creditor or the DNR has the power to force the company to submit additional information or answer questions in support of a chosen method of recording or disclosure. In this case, the student has additional support for catering to the prediction objective of shareholders (hence, early revenue recognition), provided full disclosure of adopted accounting policies exists.

It should be clear to students that logic and judgment are important, and are heavily stressed in this text. Many exercises, problems, and cases in this text will require the display of logic and judgment discussed above.

c. An auditor's report offers credibility to all users, but perhaps less so to long term creditors and shareholders, given *uncertainties* about the future, inherent judgments vis-a-vis estimates, etc.

An auditor's report provides the specific user with some assurance that statements are "presented fairly, in accordance with generally accepted accounting principles." Qualifications by the auditor often alert the user that something is going on which bears further investigation. However, it should be clear to the student that an unqualified audit opinion provides a specific user with no guarantee that the statements cater to his/her particular decision needs. Hence, students should be alert to the need for carefully worded notes to the financial statements on significant accounting policies (see Chapter 2). "Fairness" can only be interpreted in terms of adopted accounting policies. What is fair to one user group may not be fair to some other user group.

2 *A Look at Financial Statements*

An important objective of Chapter 2 is to familiarize students with the basic accounting equation, assets = liabilities + owners' equity. As explained in the text, this equation is the foundation of double-entry record-keeping. Any transaction which increases the left-hand side of the equation must by definition increase the right-hand side of the equation by an identical amount. The same principle applies for decreases. In addition, there are transactions which increase one asset or liability or equity and decrease another asset or liability or equity.

The problem which follows gives students practice in working with the basic accounting equation. The problem will stress the different balance sheet accounts and their meaning. Certain of the transactions in the problem will affect owners' equity. The important point to understand at this stage of the course is whether owners' equity is increased or decreased. Students are not expected to identify the transactions as revenues or expenses, or have a complete understanding of these transactions.

NEW PROBLEM 1 *(50-80 minutes)*

The following is a condensed balance sheet of GDR Ltd. as of June 30, 19x1.

Required:

a. Indicate the effect each of the ten undernoted events would have on the July 31, 19x1 balance sheet. Summarize the effect in the column titled "Balance, July 31, 19x1."

b. Prepare, in good form, a balance sheet as of July 31, 19x1.

c. Certain of the ten events have implications for the appraisal by shareholders of the performance of management. Indicate which ones and explain. Can you think of ways in which accounting information can assist GDR Ltd.'s shareholders in their appraisal of management's performance?

GDR Ltd.

	Balance 6/30/19x1	1	2	3	4	5	6	7	8	9	10	Balanc 7/31/19
Cash	$ 60,000		+10000		+3000				-2000		-1000	
Accounts receivable	38,000	+20,000										
Inventory	85,000	-16,000	-8000				30000 6000					
Prepaid Rent	3,000				5000							
Equipment	127,000				120000							
Building	301,000											
	$614,000											
Accounts payable	$ 29,000											
Wages payable	6,000											
Notes payable	57,000											
Bonds payable	225,000					50000 30000						
Common Shares	68,000											
Retained earnings	229,000	$ 4,000	2000	-1000	-2000	70000			-6000	-2000	-1000	
	$614,000											

---

1. The company sells, for $20,000, goods that had initially cost $16,000. The purchaser agrees to pay within 45 days.
2. The company sells, for $10,000 in cash, goods that had initially cost $8,000.
3. The prepaid rent balance as of June 30, 19x1 represents three months rent paid in advance. No rent is paid in cash during July.
4. The company, realizing it had made a purchasing error, sells in July (for $3,000 cash) some equipment it had paid $5,000 for on June 30, 19x1.
5. A new building is purchased, for $120,000 cash. To help finance the new building, the company issues $50,000 in long term bonds and $70,000 in common shares during July, 19x1.
6. The company purchases merchandise inventory for $30,000. The supplier is to be paid in 45 days.
7. A surprise inventory count is taken by the company's accountant on July 31, 19x1. The count reveals that $85,000 worth of merchandise inventory, at cost, is on hand.
8. Interest of $2,000 is paid to bondholders during July. Interest is payable on a monthly basis.
9. The company's accountant figures out that (ignoring depreciation expense) the company had net loss of $5,000 during the month of July 19x1.
10. Management decides to declare and pays a dividend of $1,000 to common shareholders, effective July 31, 19x1.

A Solution

This problem is slightly above average difficulty. Students who first try the problem and then study the solution stand to learn a considerable amount about the basic accounting equation and how it works. Having done this, students should have an easier time with the other exercises and problems in Chapter 2 of the text.

a. 1. This transaction should be analysed in two stages. In stage a, the company increases its assets (accounts receivable) and increases its retained earnings (sales) by $20,000. In stage b, the company decreases its assets (inventory) and decreases its retained earnings (cost of goods sold) by $16,000. The net impact is an increase in net assets of $4,000 and an increase in retained earnings of $4,000. The $4,000 figure represents the income or "profit" (sales less cost of goods which were sold) which the company made on the transaction. This income increases retained earnings, which is part of owners' equity. This will become clearer in a later chapter when the income statement is discussed. The lesson here for students is to separate out each stage of a transaction and isolate its effect on the accounting equation. Any complex transaction is just a sequence of simple transactions, each of which is analysed separately. Here, the two stages are: a., accepting a receivable and recording a sale, and b., giving up inventory and recording cost of goods sold. Eventually (in 45 days), a third stage will occur in which c., $20,000 of cash is received and the $20,000 in accounts receivable is eliminated. In terms of our accounting equation, this increases cash and decreases accounts receivable by the same amount, thus leaving assets in total unchanged.

2. Again, let us separate this transaction into two stages. The two stages are a., taking on cash of $10,000 and recording a sale of the same amount, and b., giving up inventory costing $8,000 and recording cost of goods sold of the same amount. The "profit" earned here is $2,000. The main difference between event 1. and event 2. is that event 2. involves a cash sale (the cash is received immediately), while event 1, involves a sale on account (the cash is received later and a receivable is assumed).

3. This event forces students to think about what prepaid rent represents. It is cash paid out at some previous date in order to benefit current and several future accounting periods. Thus, we refer to the expenditures as giving rise to an asset. This asset is written off to expense as time expires, in an even amount each period. Exactly one month has expired. Hence, accountants decrease assets by $1,000 and decrease retained earnings (rent expense) by $1,000. This will become clearer in Chapters 4 and 5 when expenses such as rent are matched to the revenues which they earn.

4. This transaction may initially be confusing to some students. Again, let us separate this transaction into two stages. The two stages are: 1., taking on cash of $3,000 and recording revenue from

GDR Ltd.

	Balance 6/30/19x1	Transactions 1	2	3	4	5	6	7	8	9	10	Balance 7/31/19x1
Cash	$ 60,000		+10,000		+3,000	+120,000 -120,000			-2,000		-1,000	$ 70,000
Accounts receivable	38,000	+20,000								N O		58,000
Inventory	85,000	-16,000	- 8,000				+30,000	-6,000				85,000
Prepaid rent	3,000			-1,000								2,000
Equipment	127,000				-5,000					E N		122,000
Building	301,000					+120,000				T R		421,000
	$614,000									Y		$758,000
Accounts payable	$ 29,000						+30,000					$ 59,000
Wages payable	6,000											6,000
Notes payable	57,000											57,000
Bonds payable	225,000					+ 50,000						275,000
Common shares	68,000					+ 70,000						138,000
Retained earnings	229,000	+20,000 -16,000	+10,000 - 8,000	-1,000	-2,000			-6,000	-2,000		-1,000	223,000
	$614,000											$758,000

the sale of equipment of $3,000 (hence, assets (+) and retained earn-
ings (+)); and b., giving up a fixed asset which had cost $5,000 and
recording a cost associated with the sale, of $5,000 (hence, assets (-)
and retained earnings (-)). The sale has given rise to a $2,000 "loss"
(the excess of purchased cost over proceeds of sale). As a simplify-
ing procedure, when fixed assets are disposed of, accountants often net
the amounts:

> asset (+) $5,000   retained earnings (-) $2,000
> asset (-) $3,000

5. Once again, this transaction initially seems complex. But let us
separate the transaction into its component stages. First, a building
is purchased (asset +) and cash is decreased (asset -). The financing
steps are totally separate transactions. Students often make the
mistake of lumping financing and investing transactions together.
These are best analyzed separately. Let us look at the two financing
transactions. With the bonds, the company increases cash (assets (+))
and increases bonds payable (liabilities (+)). With the common
shares, the company again increases cash (assets (+)) and this time
increases common shares (shareholders' equity (+)).

6. Here the result is assets (+) and liabilities (+). The company
increases inventory and increases accounts payable.

7. This event is known as an "inventory shortage" (the excess of what
the general ledger balance says is on hand and what is actually on
hand, at cost), computed as follows:

> Inventory - July 1, 19x1 $85,000
> Plus purchases   30,000
> Less inventory sold to customers   (24,000)
>
> Inventory - July 1, 19x1 - per
>   general ledger   91,000
>
> Inventory - July 1, 19x1 - per
>   physical count   85,000
>
> Unexplained shortage $ 6,000

Accountants give recognition to such a shortage by decreasing inventory (a "write-down") and decreasing retained earnings (hence, assets
(-) and shareholders' equity (-)). Of course, explanations are sought
(misplaced? theft? overshipment to a customer? goods never received
from a supplier but paid for?) and remedial action is taken. As a
later chapter will explain, what is called "perpetual inventory
records" and better "internal control" might have prevented such a
loss.

8. Here the result is assets (-) and shareholders' equity (-). The

company decreases its cash when interest is paid and decreases retained earnings (interest expense) at the same time.

9. This is a tricky question because it involves other ones. There is no need to record this event as it is already reflected in previous entries that have been made to our worksheet. Net income is the "result" of these entires. To see this, let us see how net income is computed:

Sales	$30,000
Cost of goods sold	24,000
Gross profit	6,000
Rent expense	1,000
Equipment loss	2,000
Inventory shortage	6,000
Interest expense	2,000
Expenses	11,000
Net loss for month	$ 5,000

The student can come back to this computation after Chapter 4 if it is not understood now.

10. Here the results are assets (-) and shareholders' equity (-). The company decreases its cash when dividends are paid and decreases its retained earnings by the same amount.

b.

GDR Ltd.

Balance Sheet as of July 31, 19x1

Assets		Equities	
Current assets:		Current liabilities:	
Cash	$ 70,000	Accounts payable	$ 59,000
Accounts receivable	58,000	Wages payable	6,000
Inventory	85,000	Notes payable	57,000
Prepaid rent	2,000		122,000
	$215,000	Bonds payable	275,000
			397,000
Long-lived:		Owners' equity:	
Equipment	122,000	Common shares	138,000
Building	421,000	Retained earnings	223,000
	543,000		361,000
	$758,000		$758,000

c. The loss on the fixed asset sale, one month after purchase, indicates a purchasing error, something the shareholders may or may not be interested in. The inventory shortage may reflect poor "internal control", a phrase which refers to the system of checks--similar to

fire and burglar alarms which are in place (such as segregation of
duties, proper records of inventory, someone to check outgoing shipments and incoming receipts, and so on). The implementation of an
appropriate system of internal controls is management's responsibility,
and shareholders may be unhappy about the loss if they knew. The
decision to declare a dividend despite a loss is not clearly good or
bad management. Declaration may be in accordance with shareholders'
wishes. An overall profit for the year may be anticipated. We just
do not know.

How can we expect shareholders to find out about the loss on disposal
and the inventory loss? Ideally, unusual items like this would be
disclosed separately in the financial statements (on the income
statement, to be precise), especially if the dollar amounts are considered significant (that is, "material"). This is especially
important if the company's shares are widely held and shareholders
lack a close familiarity with business operations. Unfortunately,
items like this often do not get disclosed because financial statements are prepared by management, which in effect is reporting on
itself. This is a dilemma which is dealt with by the authors at
various stages in the textbook. For now, suffice it to say that
accounting information does have a role to play for shareholders who
want to appraise management's performance.

TEXTBOOK *C2-1: A SOLUTION (40-60 minutes)

This question is a difficult one and might be postponed to Chapter 3 or 4.
It is here for those who have had a bookkeeping course in the past and want
to test their recall of the material. Try to complete it before starting
Chapter 5 of the textbook.

A full discussion of a "case approach" to learning accounting will be postponed until Chapter 3. (The Appendix to Chapter 5 of the text also provides an explanation of less directive learning.) This particular "case"
is more directed, less ambiguous and more highly structured (it asks for a
computation, with no reference as to the possible uses of the accounting
information) than the typical cases which appear in later chapters. The
case does have many missing facts, a situation that requires students to
make assumptions about what happened during the year. Thus, it is a step
towards the less structured cases of later chapters where students will
be required to make assumptions about (1) the possible uses of the accounting information (hence, objectives), (2) missing facts, and (3) possible
constraints (legal and other), before resolving accounting problems.

This "case" tests an understanding of the basic accounting equations
presented in Chapter 2 and a reconstruction of certain balance sheet and
income statement amounts using those equations.

To compute sales revenue for the year, the student must look to the possible balance sheet accounts which tell him what sales are for the year.
As a first step, the student might try:

Sales = 19x2 accounts receivable - 19x1 accounts receivable
+ cash received from customers during the year.

Why does this make sense? Perhaps it will be clearer for the student to
see it in another form:

Sales = 19x2 accounts receivable - (19x1 accounts receivable
- cash received from customers during the year).

Cash received from customers during the year reduces accounts receivable
outstanding. The difference between the reduced figure and the 19x2
accounts receivable balance must be due to sales for the year. This can
be illustrated in terms of (+) and (-):

Accounts Receivable

19x1 balance (+) $45,000		
(+) $95,000		$60,000 (-)
19x2 balance (+) $80,000		

The $60,000 cash collected reduces accounts receivable. This will become
known to students in the next chapter as a credit to accounts receivable.
The $95,000 must be the sales figure, which increases (debits) the accounts
receivable balance. To see that this obeys our first equation:

Closing Balance - Opening Balance + Cash collected = Sales

$80,000   - $45,000   + $60,000   = $95,000

(Note that this equation applies only to a situation involving sales and
accounts receivable. Other equations will be needed for other situations.)

Students should be aware of the assumptions that underly this answer. In
responding to the above we have assumed that:

- There are only sales on account and no sales for cash. This point will
  become clearer to students in a later chapter. A cash sale increases
  (debits) the cash account balance and increases (credits) the sales
  account balance, thus bypassing the accounts receivable account.
- There are no bad debt write-offs. Again, this may not be clear to the
  students until a later chapter. Such write-offs in effect decrease
  (credit) the accounts receivable balance and increase (debit) some
  expense account. These are reasonable assumptions for the student to
  make, since nothing in the case would indicate otherwise. They are also
  correct assumptions in the sense that they allow us to reconstruct the
  entire set of accounts (something the student is not asked to do).

To compute cost of goods sold for the year, the student must again consider which balance sheet account balances will tell her the needed information. The student might try:

Cost of goods sold = 19x1 inventory + purchases during the year
- 19x2 inventory.

The case indicates the amount of cash payments made to suppliers during the year for purchases of inventory. Since no merchandise has been purchased and not yet paid for (notice that there is no accounts payable balance as of 19x2), this must be the entire purchases for the year. Therefore,

Cost of goods sold = opening inventory balance + purchases - closing inventory balance.

= $15,000 + $35,000 - $25,000

= $25,000

To compute net income, students can use the equation presented in Chapter 2:

Shareholders' equity, September 30, 19x2 - shareholders' equity, September 30, 19x1 = Net income for the year.

This assumes there are no additional shares issued and no dividends paid during the year. Using the additional equation that assets - liabilities = shareholders' (owners') equity, we have:

Net assets, 19x2 - net assets, 19x1 = net income for the year (that is, change in net assets for the year).

The net assets figures are cash + accounts receivable + inventory + plant, property and equipment - mortgage payable. The balance at September 30, 19x1 is $125,000 ($5,000 + $45,000 + $15,000 + $100,000 - $40,000). The balance at September 30, 19x2 is $165,000.

Net income = $165,000 - $125,000 = $40,000

Finally, the shareholders' equity at September 30, 19x2 is just 19x2 net assets or $165,000. This follows from above.

How can a student check his answer? Were the assumptions that we made reasonable ones? One way to check is to see what changes in asset or liability accounts have not yet been accounted for by our analysis above. Let us start with cash:

$5,000 (19x1 balance) + $60,000 (19x2 sales) - $35,000 (purchases)
= $30,000 (19x2 balance)

Since we know the 19x2 balance is $10,000, there is a $20,000 payment not yet accounted for. For lack of a better assumption, let us assume this represents a general expense. The payment decreases (credits) cash and decreases (debits) some expense account other than cost of goods sold. Now, what about plant, property and equipment? Presumably, recorded depreciation served to decrease (credit) plant etc. and increase (debit) some expense account other than cost of goods sold. This assumes there were no additions or disposals of fixed assets during the year (a reasonable assumption). We are now in a position to "prove" our net income figure calculated previously ($40,000):

Net income = sales - cost of goods sold - other expenses - depreciation expense

$$= \$95,000 - \$25,000 - \$20,000 - \$10,000$$

$$= \$40,000$$

To complete the answer, we should point out some of the assumptions we have made implicitly:

- any interest paid on the mortgage payable was included in our $20,000 general expense figure

- no adjusting entries are required (the meaning of this will become clearer later)

- there are no other assets and liabilities

Notice the many assumptions made in the course of the above analysis. Perhaps the ones made by some students are different but still allow another student to arrive at a complete answer. Assumptions are fine as long as they are supported by the information given in the case and incorporate good judgment. The assumptions made above were the simplest ones to select given the facts. Without stating these assumptions, the answer would not be complete. This is what distinguishes this case from other problems and exercises in the chapter. Students should be alert for less-structured "case-type" questions which require assumptions. In Chapter 3, we will discuss a case (C3-1) where there is even less structure and more assumptions required than this case. Remember, accountants in practice often face loosely structured (real world) situations where assumptions are required because facts are not readily ascertainable. This is one reason such cases are used for instruction in your textbook.

3 *The Recording Process*

Chapters 3, 4, and 5 tend to form a package of what may be described as fundamental material for an understanding of the mechanics of financial accounting. In case it is of consolation to you, most students initially have difficulty with this material; all you can do is try your best. The ideas will fall into place in time as long as you exert some effort and do the assigned questions and problems. The three chapters cover double entry accrual accounting, and its differences from cash basis accounting.

Before commencing New Problem 1, let us review some terminology.

Debit	Credit
Increases an asset	Decreases an asset
Decreases a liability	Increases a liability
Decreases owner's equity	Increases owner's equity
Increases expenses	Decreases expenses
Decreases revenue	Increases revenue

Problem 1. concentrates on the nature of transactions which are given recognition in journal entries. A journal entry is recorded when a cheque or cash is received or issued, or when both parties to a contract meet their obligation; or when circumstances to be described later in the book occur. It is important to grasp when an entry is necessary and when it is not. The problem also gives practice in labelling accounts, making journal entries, posting them, preparing financial statements, and interpreting them. It may take longer than the 60-80 minutes we have noted as an appropriate solution time if you think out your response.

It may be helpful to review the financial statements in Chapters 2 and 3 of the textbook, concentrating on the titles given to accounts and the form of financial statements. Problem 1. is a proprietorship. See especially pages 92 to 97 of the textbook, *CFA*, for the format of owner's equity in a proprietorship.

In New Problem 2., we also illustrate the fundamental accounting cycle, from journal entries right through to the preparation of an income statement and balance sheet. This problem is similar to 1., but is provided to give extra practice to those who could use help. Concepts such as the design of a general ledger system (the tradeoff between having several accounts and separate information and the incurring of additional accounting/bookkeeping preparation costs) are touched on. The resulting financial statements are then used to facilitate, perhaps, a loan decision by a prospective lender, who is deemed to want cash flow (cash receipts less disbursements) information about the future. (Will the lender receive her money back?) Students should note that the preparation of a trial balance is not required by Problem 2. However, for practice, they may want to prepare one from the T-account information.

NEW PROBLEM 1 (60-80 minutes)

Darlene's Mini-mart (DM) commenced operations on September 1, 19x1. During the month of September, 19x1, the following transactions and events occurred:

September 1: A bank account was opened in the name of Darlene's Mini-mart and $20,000 cash was deposited by Darlene Brown.

September 2: Arrangements were made with the bank to obtain a bank loan of $30,000 on September 20, 19x1.

September 3: A lease was signed on a small store; a cheque for $1,600 was issued against DM's bank account; $400 was paid for September's rent; and a deposit of $1,200 was given to the owner of the store. The deposit will be used to pay for the last three month's rent of the lease, which requires three month's notice to cancel.

September 4: Groceries costing $18,000 were ordered from a food wholesaler; a cheque for $8,000 was issued and a promise was made to pay the remaining $10,000 on September 20. Delivery of the groceries is scheduled for September 13.

September 5: A long-term contract was signed with a supplier of store equipment (shelves; cash register; freezers; etc.). Monthly rental is $1,000; a cheque for $1,000 for September was issued. Also a cheque for $900 was issued to an installer of the equipment.

September 6: Advertising for the store opening on September 15 was arranged. The cost is to be $800; a cheque for $500 was issued to a printer to prepare brochures; another cheque for $200 was written to a distributing company; and the other $100 cheque went to an advertising consultant.

September 7: A cheque for $5,000 was issued to another food wholesaler for goods to be delivered on September 13 and 14.

September 8-30: During this time the following occurred:
- The bank loan of $30,000 was received.
- The $10,000 was paid to the food wholesaler.
- The deliveries of groceries occurred on the dates stated above.
- Various business expenses of $1,350, pertaining to September, were paid by cheque (heat, light, etc.).
- Wages of $400 were paid to a store clerk for work performed in September. The proprietor of DM, Ms. Brown, did not pay herself any wages.
- Groceries were sold for cash of $11,550.
- Another $3,500 was paid by cheque to various suppliers (of bread, cakes, milk, and other items, delivered on a daily basis to DM).

September 30: The inventory of unsold groceries was counted and costed as of the close of business on September 30 and showed the cost as approximately $17,300.

Required:

a. Prepare journal entries for the September transactions. (Indicate any assumptions which you have made.)
b. Post the journal entries to ledger T-accounts.
c. Prepare a trial balance at September 30, 19x1.
d. Prepare an income statement for September, 19x1.
e. Prepare a balance sheet as of September 30, 19x1.
f. Is DM successful?

A Solution

a. Required Journal Entries: (Those entries which are to be posted to ledger T-accounts are numbered 1., 2., 3., etc. Ones not numbered are illustrations of alternative accounting treatments.)

September 1:   1. Cash in bank (asset +) $20,000
                   Darlene Brown, Capital (owner's
                     equity +) $20,000
                   To record issuance of capital and
                   deposit of cash in a bank.

September 2: No entry is made at this point because only a promise exists and the promise does not become effective until September 20. No cash has been received; the transaction does not become effective until September 20 when both parties to the transaction exchange agreements: The bank provides the money and DM agrees to pay the money back at a later date.

September 3: This transaction is a little trickier than the previous two. The $1,600 represents an asset as of September 3. But, by the end of September, $400 of the $1,600 will be an expense. Generally, when accountants know that financial statements will not be prepared until a certain date (in this case September 30), they will expense a sum now, even though it is not an expense until later. $400 is the amount of the September rent and is therefore an expense. The remaining $1,200 is an asset, usually called a "prepaid expense" or "prepaid rent", and will become an expense at some future date. Hence, as of September 3, an appropriate journal entry is:

2. Rent expense (expense +) $ 400
    Prepaid rent (asset +)   1,200
        Cash in bank (asset –) $1,600
    To record issuance of a cheque
    for September rent and for a
    $1,200 deposit.

September 4: On the surface, this transaction may seem similar to that on September 2 (i.e., "delivery" occurs in the future). However, there is an important difference. On September 4 we are issuing a cheque for $8,000; hence, we will have to record this. A suitable entry might be:

3. Deposit on purchase of inventory
        (asset +) $8,000
        Cash in bank (asset –) $8,000
    To record issuance of deposit
    cheque.

In practice, because delivery is expected before the end of September (when financial statements are to be prepared), the following journal entry *might* be made in place of 3.:

    Inventory (asset +) $18,000
        Cash in bank (asset –) $ 8,000
        Accounts payable (liability +)   10,000
    To record purchase of inventory.

When the goods are received, no journal entry would be made because a debit to inventory (or goods for resale) already exists. However, when the account payable is paid, the journal entry would be:

    Accounts payable (liability –) $10,000
        Cash in bank (asset –) $10,000
    To record payment of liability.

September 5: Two events have occurred on this date. The first is the issuance of a cheque for $1,000 and is similar to the September 3 transaction. A suitable entry would be:

4. Equipment rental expense
        (expense +) $ 1,000
        Cash in bank (asset –) $ 1,000
    To record issuance of cheque for
    rentals.

No entry is necessary to acknowledge the signing of a long-term contract unless DM is in effect buying the equipment under a long-term lease. This complication is discussed in Chapter 10 of your textbook.

The second transaction, for $900 of installation costs, might be handled by accountants in one of two ways. They could record the $900 as an expense:

    5.   Installation expense (expense +) $ 900
           Cash in bank (asset -) $ 900
         To record payment for the installation.

This method then charges September for all of the cost of $900. Some may regard this as being unfair because the equipment helps to generate revenue over many months; not just September, 19x1. Hence, other accountants might use this treatment on September 5:

       Installation cost (asset +) $ 900
         Cash in bank (asset -) $ 900
       To record payment for the installation.

Observe that the word "cost" tends to refer to assets.

As the asset is used up over the period of the lease (in much the same way as some assets depreciate), the following journal entry would be appropriate each month. (It is assumed that the lease is for 90 months.):

       Installation expense (expense +) $ 10
         Installation cost (asset -) $ 10
       To record monthly expense.

This approach might better match expenses with revenue. But, as we will see in Chapter 5, there is often more to consider.

September 6: Since cheques have been issued, and the advertising brochures will be distributed before September 30 (the date when financial statements are to be prepared), accountants typically regard advertising as an expense:

    6.   Advertising expense (expense +) $ 800
           Cash in bank (asset -) $ 800
         To record payment of an expense.

We could have three credits to "cash in bank"; this matter is discussed in later chapters. Advertising is not usually treated as an asset because it is usually not possible to measure whether it has significant usefulness in future periods.

September 7: This entry is similar to that for September 4:

```
         7.  Deposit on purchase of
             inventory (asset +)              $ 5,000
                Cash in bank (asset -)                       $ 5,000
             To record deposit on inventory.
```

September 8-30: A series of journal entries are necessary, and will
be taken in order per the question.

```
         8.  Cash in bank (asset +)           $30,000
                Bank loan payable (liability +)             $30,000
             To record receipt of bank loan.


         9.  Inventory (asset +)              $10,000
                Cash in bank (asset -)                      $10,000
             To record receipt of inventory
             and payment for same.
```

Some may wish to credit an account payable first and later debit it,
in place of 9. The net effect, though, is the same.

```
        10.  Inventory (asset +)              $13,000
                Deposit on purchase of
                inventory (asset -)                         $13,000
             To record receipts from two sup-
             pliers; one for $8,000 and a second
             for $5,000.
```

Entry 10. might also be in two parts. When the inventory is received
on September 13, for example, the entry would be:

```
             Inventory (asset +)             $23,000
                Accounts payable (liability +)              $10,000
                Deposit on purchase of
                inventory (asset +)                         $13,000
             To record receipt of inventory.
```

When the payable is paid the entry would be:

```
             Accounts payable (liability -)  $10,000
                Cash in bank (asset -)                      $10,000
             To record payment of liability.


        11.  Miscellaneous expense (expense +) $1,350
                Cash in bank (asset -)                       $1,350
             To record various expenses.


        12.  Wages expense (expense +)        $  400
                Cash in bank (asset -)                       $  400
             To record wages for September.


        13.  Cash in bank (asset +)           $11,550
                Revenue (revenue +)                         $11,550
             To record sales and bank deposit.
```

14.   Inventory (asset +) $3,500
            Cash in bank (asset −) $3,500
            To record purchase of inventory.

September 30: We are told that DM purchased the following inventory for resale: $18,000 + $5,000 + $3,500 for a total of $26,500. We are also told that $17,300 remains at the end of September. Thus, $9,200 must have been sold (or sold and stolen). The entry to relieve the asset account and charge an expense is:

15.   Cost of goods sold (expense +) $9,200
            Inventory (asset +) $9,200
            To record cost of goods sold.

b. Posting to ledger accounts:

Assets		Liabilities and owner's capital (including revenues and expenses)	

Cash in bank

1)	20,000	(2)	1,600
8)	30,000	(3)	8,000
13)	11,550	(4)	1,000
		(5)	900
		(6)	800
		(7)	5,000
		(9)	10,000
		(11)	1,350
		(12)	400
		(14)	3,500
29,000			

Prepaid rent

2)	1,200		
1,200			

Deposit on purchase of inventory

3)	8,000	(10)	13,000
7)	5,000		

Inventory

9)	10,000	(15)	9,200
10)	13,000		
14)	3,500		
17,300			

Darlene Brown, capital

	(1) 20,000
	20,000

Rent expense

(2)	400	
400		

Miscellaneous expense

(11) 1,350	
1,350	

Cost of goods sold

(15) 9,200	
9,200	

Advertising expense

(6)	800	
800		

Bank loan payable

	(8) 30,000
	30,000

Equipment rental expense

(4) 1,000	
1,000	

Wages expense

(12)	400	
400		

Installation expense

(5)	900	
900		

Revenue

	(13) 11,550
	11,550

c. Trial Balance:

	Debits	Credits
Cash in bank	$29,000	
Prepaid rent	1,200	
Inventory	17,300	
Darlene Brown, capital		$20,000
Bank loan payable		30,000
Rent expense	400	
Equipment rental expense	1,000	
Miscellaneous expense	1,350	
Wages expense	400	
Cost of goods sold	9,200	
Installation expense	900	
Advertising expense	800	
Revenue		11,550
	$61,550	$61,550

d. Income Statement:

Darlene's Mini-mart

Income Statement

From Commencement of the Business Until

September 30, 19x1

Revenue		$11,550
Expenses:		
Cost of goods sold	$9,200	
Equipment rental	1,000	
Miscellaneous	1,350	
Installation	900	
Advertising	800	
Rent expense	400	
Wages expense	400	14,050
Loss		$ 2,500

e. Balance Sheet:

Darlene's Mini-mart

Balance Sheet
September 30, 19x1

Assets

Cash	$29,000
Inventory	17,300
Prepaid rent	1,200
	$47,500

Liability and Owner's Capital

Bank loan payable		$30,000
Owner's capital:		
Initial investment	$20,000	
Loss for September	2,500	17,500
		$47,500

f. Is DM successful?

This question cannot be answered from the information which was made available to us. On the surface the company lost $2,500 in September. However, the following points should be kept in mind:

1. September was the first month of operations and some potential customers may not be aware of the store's existence.

2. Some start-up costs were charged to September: Advertising $800, and Installation $900. These costs may be less or not exist in future months.

3. The owner did not pay herself. When she does, "expenses" increase.

4. Interest will have to be paid on the bank loan; this will increase expenses. (Chapter 4 covers this point.)

Maybe the $2,500 loss is less than was expected (or budgeted). A longer time period is needed to form an opinion about success.

NEW PROBLEM 2 (60-80 minutes)

Madden T-Shirt Ltd. began operations on January 1, 19x5, with the intention of selling custom designed T-shirts to customers. During the first month of operations, the following events took place:

1. The company issued 100 common shares at $100 per share on January 2, 19x5. Ms. Madden purchased all of the shares, using her entire savings.

2. The company rented a store for $400 per month. It paid the first month's rent on January 3, 19x5.

3. The company purchased inventory for $5,000 cash (3,000 T-shirts at $1.00 each; ink for $1,000; and other supplies for $1,000). The supplier refused to give the new company credit until a record of several cash payments was established.

4. To conserve scarce cash, the company decided to rent its main piece of equipment, a dye printer, for $5,000 a month, commencing January 1, 19x5.

5. On January 31, 19x5, Ms. Madden paid herself $1,500, representing one month's salary. On the same date, she borrowed $500 from the company with the intention of paying it back the following month.

6. Advertisements were arranged with local newspapers, at a cost of $1,000, payable in cash on January 15, 19x5. The ads were to run for a full year, commencing in February, 19x5.

7. Ms. Madden agreed to purchase her lunches for January, 19x5, worth $25 a week, across the street, in exchange for "free" T-shirts to the staff of the restaurant.

8. Cash received from customers during the first month of operations amounted to $4,000. Ms. Madden was pleased, and felt her goal of $96,000 sales for the year was attainable.

9. A friend suggested Ms. Madden record some depreciation on the machine which she rented, for the month of January, to reflect its decline in useful life.

10. Ms. Madden took end-of-month inventory on January 31, 19x5 and found she had 1,950 T-shirts, one-half of the ink supply, and one-half of other supplies on hand.

11. Knowing that cash flow (cash receipts less cash disbursements) would be a problem, Ms. Madden approached a friend and asked for a loan to the company of $10,000, payable at the end of the first year of operations.

Required:

a. Prepare journal entries to record the transactions of the first month of operations. (Indicate any assumptions which you have made.)
b. Post the journal entries to ledger T-accounts.
c. Prepare an income statement for the month.
d. Prepare any closing entries that would be necessary if the books were to be closed at the end of the month. (Ordinarily, books would be closed only at the end of a full accounting period, usually one year.)
e. Prepare a statement of position (a balance sheet).
f. As a friend who was approached, would you lend the company the requested $10,000? Why or why not?

At this stage of the course it is essential that you do the question before viewing the solution. Quick feedback aids the learning process.

A Solution

a.
                                                                    (1)

Cash in bank (asset +) $10,000
   Common shares (owner's equity +) $10,000
To record initial cash contribution and issue
of common shares.

Rent expense (expense +) $ 400
  Cash (assets -) $ 400
To record the payment of one month's rent.

(3)

Inventory, T-shirts (asset +) $3,000
  Cash (asset -) $3,000

(4)

Inventory, ink (asset +) $1,000
  Cash (asset -) $1,000

(5)

Inventory, other (asset +) $1,000
  Cash (asset -) $1,000
To record the purchase of inventories.

(These three could be combined into one journal entry, especially if the cash payment is made to one supplier, instead of three, as the question indicates.)

Students should note an important fact about entries (3), (4), and (5). Three separate Inventory accounts are created, rather than one account entitled "inventory." This leads us to an important question: how many general ledger accounts should be created for one item such as inventory? The answer is a matter of judgment, and will vary with the complexity of the business, the information needs of management and owners, the nature of the item in question, and so on. Here, we have a simple one-product line business with three basic categories of supplies. The owner-manager, Ms. Madden needs to keep track of each inventory category, as each is expensive in terms of her business. Therefore, it makes sense to open three separate general ledger accounts, one for each category. On the other hand, had there been two hundred types of supplies, most of them minor dollar value, it might make sense to lump them into one, two or more categories for ease of bookkeeping purposes. The tradeoff is better internal control (better records of what was purchased and used) versus higher bookkeeping/accounting costs. A cost/benefit analysis may be useful. This is discussed later in the textbook.

(6)

Equipment rental expense (expense +) $5,000
  Cash (asset -) $5,000
To record the cost of monthly equipment rental.

Students should notice that we have used a separate rental expense account to distinguish this expense from building rental, for the same reasons as discussed for the previous three journal entries.

(7)

Salary expense (expense +) $1,500
  Cash (asset −) $1,500
To record salary paid to Ms. Madden.

For simplicity's sake, this problem ignores personal income tax and other deductions which, according to law, must be deducted by the company from the gross wage paid to an employee. In later chapters, these complexities will be explained in the textbook and introduced into some problems.

(8)

Loan to shareholder (asset +) $ 800
  Cash (asset −) $ 800
To record short term loan made to Ms. Madden
by the company.

It is important that such a transaction be recorded in the general ledger, ideally in a separate general ledger account so that the item is easily kept in view. Potential creditors, the Department of National Revenue (income tax), and others, are very interested in transactions between a shareholder and the company, because the two are not operating at "arm's length" and these readers may want to assess to what extent a benefit is being conferred on the shareholder. For this reason, such loans are disclosed separately on the balance sheet. (This is further explained in Chapter 5 and later in the textbook.)

(9)

Prepaid advertising (asset +) $1,000
  Cash (asset −) $1,000
To record prepaid advertising (ads to commence
in February).

Students should be careful not to record any expense of advertising in January, since no service is performed until February when the first advertisement appears. Also note that the expense will be recognized as each advertisement appears, rather than evenly over time as is the case for rent expense. The lesson here is that for accounting purposes, the benefit of this type of service arises at one point in time (when the ad appears), rather than evenly over a period of time. Accountants are not able to measure the exact time when advertising has effect and generates benefits. Hence, they tend to expense the cash outlays for advertising when the ads appear.

(10)

Withdrawals by owner (owner's equity −)	$ 100	
Cash (asset −)		$ 100

(11)

Cash (asset +)	$ 100	
Sales, T-shirts (owner's equity +; or revenue +)		$ 100

To record meals purchased in exchange for T-shirts.

The topic of "barter" arrangements (service swaps between companies where no cash changes hands) is a difficult one, and students should not be discouraged if they do not grasp it at this point. The reason for giving this situation is to force the student to think in terms of substance rather than the form of a transaction. In substance, Ms. Madden is selling T-shirts to the restaurant, and receiving services (meals) worth $100 a month instead of cash for them. It may help for learning purposes to view her as (1) having received the cash and (2) having purchased the meals; that is, as having accomplished two transactions.

(This is the way the Income Tax assessors would tend to view the arrangement.) Notice that we have made a complex transaction seem easier once we looked at the separate stages.

A second issue is involved, which is distinguishing personal expenses (such as lunches) from company expenses. A "fine line" sometimes exists between the two. Although the meals might be regarded by some as a company expense, they in effect are a benefit conferred upon the sole shareholder, Ms. Madden. The benefit is something like an extra salary. Good financial disclosure would require that this benefit be reported separately in the financial statements (if it is to be treated as an expense). Such disclosure would alert financial statement readers to the existence of a "non-arm's length transaction" between a shareholder and the company. The reader of the financial statements may then decide for himself whether the transaction was reasonable. The credit to sales in (11) is labelled as owner's equity +, because the $100 less the cost of the shirts sold (less any other related expenses) would increase owner's equity.

(12)

Cash (asset +)	$4,000	
Sales, T-shirts (owner's equity +; or revenue +)		$4,000

To record sales for the month.

Note that these are cash sales, and no accounts receivable are involved.

No entry is required to reflect depreciation on the rented machine. The comment in the question is a "trap." Although depreciation accounting is not covered in depth until a later chapter, you may have realized that a company does not depreciate an asset which it does not (in substance) own. In this question, we have a simple rental arrangement; the rental company depreciates the equipment on its books.

(13)

Cost of goods sold (owner's equity -;
  or expense +) $2,050
    Inventory, T-shirts (asset -) $1,050
    Inventory, ink (asset -) $ 500
    Inventory, other (asset -) $ 500
To record the cost of T-shirts that were sold.

Entry (13) is called an adjusting entry, a topic which is discussed at length in Chapter 4. The credits to "inventory" in (13) are made to reduce the amount shown in the three inventory ledger accounts to the sum on hand at January 31, 19x5. For example, only $1,950 of the T-shirt inventory exists at January 31, 19x5. Yet, as a result of jornal entry (3), the ledger account for T-shirt inventory would show $3,000. Entry (13) reduces (or adjusts) the $3,000 to $1,950 by making a credit of $1,050.

b. The journal entries would be posted to the various ledger accounts (closing entries are also shown, as C1, or C2):

Assets				Liabilities and shareholder's equity			

Cash in bank

(1)	10,000	(2)	400
(11)	100	(3)	3,000
(12)	4,000	(4)	1,000
		(5)	1,000
		(6)	5,000
		(7)	1,500
		(8)	800
		(9)	1,000
		(10)	100
	14,100		13,800
	300		

Prepaid advertising

(9)	1,000	

Inventory, T-shirts

(3)	3,000	(13)	1,050
	1,950		

Inventory, ink

(4)	1,000	(13)	500
	500		

Inventory, other

(5)	1,000	(13)	500
	500		

Loan to shareholder

(8)	800	

Common shares

		(1)	10,000

Rent expense, building

(2)	400	(C2)	400

Rent expense, equipment

(6)	5,000	(C2)	5,000

Retained earnings

(C3)	4,850		
(C4)	100		
	4,950		

Salary expense

(7)	1,500	(C2)	1,500

Withdrawals by owner

(10)	100	(C4)	100

Sales, T-shirts

(C1)	4,100	(11)	100
		(12)	4,000

Cost of goods sold

(13)	2,050	(C2)	2,050

Income summary

		(C1)	4,100
(C2)	400		
(C2)	5,000		
(C2)	1,500		
(C2)	2,050		
	8,950		4,100
		(C3)	4,850

- 39 -

c.

Madden T-Shirt Ltd.

Income Statement

Month Ended January 31, 19x5

Revenues		
T-shirt sales		$4,100
Expenses		
Rent expense, building	$ 400	
Rent expense, equipment	5,000	
Salary	1,500	
Cost of goods sold	2,050	8,950
Loss for month		($4,850)

d.

Closing entry 1

Sales, T-shirts	$4,100	
Income summary		$4,100
To close sales account.		

Closing entry 2

Income summary	$8,950	
Rent expense, building		400
Rent expense, equipment		5,000
Salary expense		1,500
Cost of goods sold		2,050
To close expense accounts.		

Closing entry 3

Retained earnings	$4,850	
Income summary		$4,850
To record the loss for the month.		

Closing entry 4

Retained earnings	$ 100	
Withdrawals by owner		$ 100
To close the "withdrawals" account		
(which is similar to a dividend) to		
retained earnings.		

The withdrawal is really a dividend or repayment to the owner, under the assumption which we made in entry (10). Alternatively, it could have been assumed to be an expense, similar to salary expense, and recorded as such.

The latter treatment would increase the loss for January 19x5 to $4,950. The $100 would be reported separately in the financial statements.

e.   Madden T-Shirt Ltd.

                              Balance Sheet

                            January 31, 19x5

                                 Assets

Current Assets
        Cash in bank $ 300
        Inventory of T-shirts   1,950
        Inventory of ink   500
        Inventory of other   500
        Loan to shareholder   800
        Prepaid advertising   1,000
                                                        $5,050

                          Shareholder's Equity

Shareholder's equity
    Common shares $10,000
    Deficit: Loss for the month $4,850
             Withdrawal or dividend   100*   (4,950)
                                                        $ 5,050

Note that accountants refer to negative retained earnings as a
"deficit."

f. Should the friend loan Madden T-Shirts Ltd. $10,000, repayable on
    December 31, 19x5? This question encourages students to take the
    creditor's perspective and use financial accounting and other infor-
    mation to aid in the loan decision. First, let us imagine that the
    friend had access only to the above income statement and balance
    sheet. What do they tell the friend? First, there is a loss for the
    month. Since this is an excess of cash outflow over cash inflow, the
    friend has good reason to be concerned. Will an increase in sales in
    the next eleven months offset this loss trend? Second, the salary to
    the shareholder is apparently generous given the results of the com-
    pany. As a potential creditor, the friend may be concerned about this
    (perhaps feeling he/she should be repaid before any salary is paid).
    Third, looking to the balance sheet, there is a positive "working
    capital" picture (excess of current assets over current liabilities).
    However, this will quickly be eliminated if the current rate of loss
    continues.

---

*This transaction may not have been legal because it reduced common share
capital, probably without creditor approval. If it is salary it should
be shown as an expense. If it is a loan, it should be a receivable.
Chapters 11 and 12 explain the issue.

Recall that in Chapter 1 we explained that creditors often have the special power to request additional information from companies. Suppose our potential creditor asks for a cash flow (cash receipts and disbursements) projection for the year. It *might* look as follows: (We have pulled figures "out of the air" for the following; in practice, we would make our best estimates.)

Madden T-Shirt Ltd.

Cash Budget

Year ended December 31, 19x5

Cash receipts:
T-shirt sales		$96,000
Loan, if made		10,000
		106,000

Cash disbursements:
Rent expense, building	$ 4,800	
Rent expense, equipment	60,000	
Employee meals	1,200 (?)	
Cost of goods sold	24,600	
Salary	*	90,600

Excess of cash receipts over cash disbursements (available for salary plus repayment of the $10,000 loan) — $15,400

(?) – This figure may be only $100 if only January is involved.

 * – Assumed to be zero just to see whether sufficient cash would exist to repay the loan.

Based on the above, the friend probably would not want to loan the company $10,000. This is because only $5,400 is available for salary and $10,000 for the loan repayment. Can Madden T-Shirt Ltd. find other cash (financing) instead? Would someone else buy common shares? What is the longer term outlook for sales? What risks (of loss of the $10,000) are involved? These questions cannot be answered from a typical balance sheet and income statement, which is for past periods.

TEXTBOOK* C3-1: A SOLUTION (75-100 minutes)

This is a difficult problem and could be postponed until Chapter 5 or later. It is placed here for those who want to be better prepared in analysis.

In Chapter 2 we discussed C2-1, which was a highly structured case with considerable direction. The case we will now discuss, C3-1, is a more difficult one than C2-1. It requires the student to think about the needs of users, the design of a record keeping system, the loan decision facing creditors, etc. To help the student get acquainted with the case approach, the cases in the early chapters have "requireds" which contain

considerable direction for the student. In later chapters, less help
will be given in the required section.

The required to C3-1 is intended to guide students logically through an
answer. The framework is a useful one. (The solution given below does
not correspond procedurally with the "required" on page 119 of the textbook.) First, we consider what sort of record keeping system and which
financial statements we want. This is the job of an accounting advisor.
Once this design stage is complete, the bookkeeper can take over.
Before any worthwhile design can take place, we must consider what uses
will be made of the record keeping system and financial statements.
That is, we consider the objectives of accounting information. To do
this, we must look to the needs of the users of ISL's financial statements and to the needs of management, the preparers of financial statements. In this case, we refer to the creditor as a user of the financial statements of ISL, and to Mr. Moss (the owner/manager) as the
"preparer." Both the user and preparer "use" the financial statements,
and the needs of both make up our uses (hence, objectives) of accounting
information. We make the distinction between user and preparer because
the latter usually has more direct influence on the design and content
of accounting information. That is, the accounting advisor reports to
Mr. Moss, who has the final say on any accounting problem. The accounting advisor also considers the needs of external users such as the bank
because the company needs a loan, and will want to present credible,
factual accounting information that helps obtain that loan.

Once the objectives of accounting information are decided upon, the
"required" part of this question then guides the student step-by-step
through case analysis. Let us stand back and look at the various
problems facing ISL's accounting advisor (all are alluded to by the
"required"):

1. Which financial statements (the balance sheet, income statement,
    statement of changes in financial position, and statement of
    retained earnings are the four main statements) should be prepared?

2. What design of a record keeping system should be chosen? That is,
    how many separate general ledger accounts should there be, what
    sorts of journals should be used to summarize transactions (a general
    journal, perhaps special journals such as a sales journal, a journal
    of cash receipts and disbursements, etc.)? Chapter 3 does not dis-
    cuss the use of journals to any great extent. A later chapter will
    introduce these concepts. For now, suffice it to say that, where a
    great many similar transactions occur, it makes sense to record
    such transactions (sales, purchases, cash receipts and disbursements)
    in a summary journal and then post only column totals to the general
    ledger. Chapter 3 of the text discusses a general journal, where
    journal entries are made. The general journal and the special
    journal are the sources from which postings are made to a general
    ledger. If there were only a few transactions, perhaps only a general
    journal would be necessary as a source for posting to the general
    ledger.

3. Having decided on design of the accounting records, we can assume that the bookkeeper is able to take the transactions and make the necessary journal entries, post to the general ledger, prepare a trial balance, make closing entries, and draw up the requested financial statements.

4. It is then the task of the accounting advisor to interpret the accounting information, perhaps for the owner who is here concerned about a "shortage of cash."

5. The company needs a loan, and the accounting advisor may be called upon to prepare a special report for a creditor (recall in Chapter 1 that we explained that creditors often have the power to request such reports).

6. A final problem entails some management accounting considerations; students will not be expected in later cases to identify these as relevant problems unless directed to do so by the required. From time to time, requirements will request students to consider internal information needs of management (the area of concern of management accounting) when it is logical to do so. This may occur when a record keeping system is being designed, as is the case here. It makes sense, in designing a general ledger, to also consider the internal decision needs of Mr. Moss (such as performance appraisal, pricing and so on).

Let us summarize before proceeding to an answer. C3-1 has a fairly directed required because we are at an early stage in the course. Later cases will be less directed. Let us now formally state a framework for case analysis, one that can be used to answer many types of cases:

1. Consider the possible objectives of accounting information which seem to be relevant in the situation. Choose relevant objectives from the following list (see also Chapter 5 of the textbook):

   (a) To assist shareholders and others who want to predict long run cash flows and earning trends (the prediction objective).
   (b) To assist creditors and others who want to assess short run cash flows (the liquidity assessment objective).
   (c) To assist shareholders and perhaps creditors in assessing management's stewardship over assets entrusted to it. (That is, can the cash loaned or invested to management be "accounted for"? Where did the cash go? This is a stewardship objective.)
   (d) To assist shareholders in appraising management's performance, perhaps for the purpose of a bonus calculation or to aid the hire/fire decision (the performance evaluation objective). Users of financial statements have to be careful with this objective because management may want to present its performance in the best light.

(e) To assist management in keeping track of assets, preventing theft and so on (the internal control objective).

(f) To assist management in deciding how much income it wants to measure and declare for income tax purposes (the income tax objective). Income for tax purposes is often affected by accounting decisions.

(g) To assist some external user in assessing compliance with some statute or legal requirement, such as the requirements of the Canada Business Corporations Act or perhaps some special contract (the compliance objective).

2. Rank the objectives in order of assumed importance in the case at hand.

3. Consider the role you are placed in (sometimes accounting advisor, sometimes bookkeeper, sometimes controller, sometimes even auditor). The responsibilities, needs and biases of each of these people might be quite different.

4. Identify and rank accounting problems, in order of importance. (Is the compliance objective more important than, say, a liquidity assessment?)

5. Analyse each problem, concentrating on the most important problems. Where possible, consider alternatives to a solution and evaluate these in light of assumed objectives, assumed and given facts, and assumed "constraints." Logic and judgment are crucial at this point. Be aware of possible conflicts in objectives. Perhaps some alternative suits one objective well and another very poorly. The alternative which best suits the most important objective should be chosen.

6. Prepare recommendations on each problem, referring where possible to assumed objectives and how the alternative selected best suits that objective.

The above is just one of several valid frameworks for approaching case analysis. It is one which we will tend to use in discussing cases, and we recommend it for your consideration. The "solution" to C3-1 which follows uses this framework and is just one of several valid responses. There is no one right answer to a case, but there are good approaches and bad approaches. Cases allow different but valid approaches because they allow different but valid assumptions regarding objectives, facts, and constraints and because equally intelligent accounting advisors may choose different solutions to problems. What is important is whether your assumptions are reasonable (in light of the facts given); whether your solution follows logically from your assumptions and analyses; whether your analysis considers alternatives and evaluates them in light of objectives/facts/constraints; and finally, whether your recommendations "do the job." That is, would they work, do they solve the problem, would management accept them?

Step 1: Objectives of accounting information (to facilitate):
a. Loan decision by creditor (hence, information needed on cash flows).
b. Internal control (to prevent lost records, and so on).
c. Income tax return preparation.

The above are ranked in order of importance. Less important are steward-ship and performance appraisal because Mr. Moss is both owner and manager.

It should be noted that one month's financial statements would not adequately satisfy any of these objectives. A decision maker (e.g., creditor) would consider a longer time frame and would use other sources of information to supplement the monthly statements. Special purpose reports might provide details of major expected cash inflows and outflows.

The above ranking places the needs of creditors above other objectives. This makes sense, as the operation may need the loan to survive. Hence, the accounting system must generate information on cash flows. Better internal control ranks as a very important second objective. With better record keeping, Mr. Moss will be better able to keep track of cash. A creditor might even insist on this system before granting a loan. A third objective, but not as important, is to keep income tax preparation needs in mind when designing a system of accounts. That is, separate records are needed for some types of expenditures (fixed assets, by major type, for example).

Step 2: The objectives are ranked above.

Step 3: The roles, as accounting advisor to Mr. Moss, and as bookkeeper, are clearly established in the "required."

Step 4: Accounting problems are identified and ranked in order of importance as follows:
a. Design of a bookkeeping or record-keeping system.
b. Which statements to prepare.
c. Problems facing the bookkeeper in preparing the statements. (Advice may be needed from the accounting advisor, your other role, to help resolve these):
    (i)   Distinguishing between shareholder's personal expenses and those of the company or entity.
    (ii)   Accounting for incorporation costs.
    (iii) Accounting for assets contributed by the shareholder in return for shares.
    (iv)   Decision to set up supplies as an asset or expense them; and adjust to physical count of goods at period end.
    (v)   Accounting for gain on sale of land – measure cost?
                                              – extraordinary item?
    (vi)   Need to accrue for wages.
d. Interpretation of financial statements. What happened to the cash?
e. Information which the accounting advisor may want to provide in a special report for the creditor.
f. Which accounting information should be prepared for which operating decisions?

<u>Step 5:</u> The analysis of problems will proceed in order of importance.
a. In designing a record keeping system, objectives/facts/constraints
    must be considered first.
    The objectives for such a record keeping system are:
    (i)   monitor cash flows (timely information is needed on cash
          balances).
    (ii) internal control (prevent loss of records, and so on).
    (iii) income tax return preparation.
    Facts – cash shortage indicates need for a timely record keeping
            system to keep track of cash, facilitating 1. and 2.
          – operations are simple.
    Constraints – ISL needs a simple system consistent with its needs.
                  An elaborate general ledger information system may not
                  be warranted.
    Consistent with the above objectives/facts/constraints, the following
    might be appropriate for ISL:
    – one general journal will suffice (special journals like a disburse-
      ment journal, voucher register, etc. would be cumbersome and super-
      fluous for a simple operation).
    – a general ledger with at least enough detail in number of accounts
      to reveal:
          – type of fixed assets owned (for tax purposes)
          – each major expense item (to monitor cash outflows and income
            tax deductibility).
    – certain expense items such as supplies should be set up as an asset,
      to help facilitate internal control. Otherwise, management tends to
      lose track of such things.
    – postings should be done at least weekly to provide the owner with
      timely information, especially given the critical cash shortage.
      More frequent postings may not be practical. ISL can bring in a
      bookkeeper once a week and an accounting advisor (for income tax,
      etc.) annually.
    Students should notice how the above ties system design considerations
    to the assumed objective of ISL.

b. A monthly balance sheet and income statement might help keep track of
    cash and might facilitate the creditor's needs. In addition, a
    monthly statement of change in financial position (stressing *cash*)
    would help owner and creditor see where cash is going. Special
    purpose reports (cash budget) would be helpful to a banker and to
    the owner and perhaps could be prepared by the bookkeeper on a
    weekly basis.

c. (i) The portion related to Moss' divorce is a personal expense. One
    can either set up a receivable from Moss' shareholder account for
    that portion, or assume it is paid out of Moss' personal funds. If
    it is assumed that the company pays, a separate account for the share-
    holder loan facilitates the income tax objective and will satisfy the
    banker. Students should note that considerable freedom for assump-
    tions exists; this is typical of many cases.
    (ii) A discussion of accounting for incorporation costs can be deferred
    until later chapters (e.g., if material in amount it might be

capitalized to facilitate matching). This was touched upon briefly in Chapter 2. This outlay does create an "asset" in the sense that the expenditure benefits many accounting periods, really the entire life of the company. If the dollar amount is significant (that is, "material"), it would not be appropriate to charge the entire amount to expense in the first year. Outlays should be written off to expense over the periods which are likely to benefit. This is called the "matching concept" to be explained in more depth in Chapter 5. For simplicity's sake, incorporation costs will be left unamortized on the first month's balance sheet of ISL; perhaps to be written off to expense at a later date when the amount is insignificant relative to total expenses.

(iii) Contributed capital is valued at the fair market value of assets contributed. This is consistent with the historic cost concept. This will be further discussed in Chapter 12.

(iv) Supplies should be initially set up as an asset and the expense portion recognized as physical inventories are taken, and it becomes possible to compute the amount of expense. This facilitates the internal control objective. The alternative, to expense such cash outlays immediately and to set up an asset when physical inventories are taken, is "dangerous" since Mr. Moss tends to lose track of such items; a balance sheet ledger account helps remind him to control his supplies.

(v) Regarding the sale of land on September 29, other allocations of cost to the land are possible, with some assumptions. Using ¼ is simple as it likely concurs with income tax measurement and does not seriously affect other objectives.

(vi) Wages must be "accrued" for the period September 27 to September 30, since workers are owed the money but have not been paid. Accruals are discussed in more depth in Chapter 4.

d. What explanation is available for the cash "shortage"? The balance sheet (Appendix C3-4) indicates a deficit of $2,200, which is owed to the bank. (This is commonly referred to as an overdraft.) It may not be cause for concern. ISL has a healthy working capital (current assets less current liabilities) position of ($59,700 - $11,580) $48,120, which should enable it to obtain a loan to meet its short term cash requirements. The loan could be repaid as current assets are converted to cash.

e. What information should be included in a special report to a potential creditor? A cash budget would be useful, prepared for the next twelve months on a monthly basis. See Problem 3-A of this chapter for an example, prepared on an annual basis. The creditor is interested in near term cash flows. He/she wants to know planned ("budgeted") sources of cash (sales, cash collections from various receivables) and planned uses of cash (cash payments to suppliers, any further additions to fixed assets, any anticipated withdrawals by the owner, or dividend payments), perhaps on a monthly basis so as to identify those months when cash will be short and a bank loan is needed. The loan might be arranged in advance of the need.

f. The important internal operating decisions are as follows:
   (i)   pricing (if ISL is able to set its own prices instead of just following others).
   (ii)   setting credit terms to conserve scarce cash.
   (iii) allocation of scarce cash to buy fixed or capital assets.
   (iv)   daily management of scarce cash.
   Accounting information can be used to facilitate such decisions. A general ledger recording system should be designed to ensure required information is available for:
   (i)   Contribution margin analysis (separate expense accounts into fixed, variable, discretionary).
   (ii)   Aging analyses, by customer, of accounts receivable (subsidiary records may be necessary).
   (iii) Capital budgeting analysis.
   (iv)   Daily statements of cash flow (special report).

Step 6: Finally, we want to prepare recommendations. In a case like Imperial Soil Limited, issues are not overly complex, and for our analysis, often just one alternative is discussed, that being the alternative that "best" fits our assumed objectives. Later in the book, cases requiring a discussion of several alternatives are provided. In later cases, issues will be more complex and often several alternatives will be considered in the analysis of each problem. In these more complex cases, it makes sense to have summary recommendations for the reader, indicating the alternative chosen and briefly stating why. In this case, the resolution to each problem is obvious from reading the analysis. Hence recommendations are omitted.

Required journal entries for C3-1:

Journal entries are as follows:

1. Land $50,000
    Tractor   5,000
    Cash   35,000
      Common shares $90,000

2. Building $10,000
      Cash $10,000

3. Accounts receivable – shareholder $ 4,000
    Incorporation costs   1,000
      Accounts payable $ 5,000

4. Equipment $ 8,000
      Cash $ 8,000

5. Supplies $10,000
      Accounts payable $10,000

6. Inventory $15,000
       Cash $10,000
       Accounts payable   5,000

7. Accounts payable $ 5,000
       Cash $ 5,000

8. Advertising expense $ 1,500
       Accounts payable $ 1,500

9. September 13: no entry required. See entries 14 and 17.

10. Accounts payable $ 5,000
       Cash $ 5,000

11. Cash $ 5,000
       Unearned revenue $ 5,000

    Having a separate account here helps Mr. Moss keep track of the
    item, thus facilitating internal control.

12. Accounts payable $ 5,000
       Cash $ 5,000

13. Cash $ 1,000
    Accounts receivable   5,000
       Sales $ 6,000

14. Wages $ 200
       Cash $ 200

15. Accounts receivable $30,000
       Gain on sale $17,500
       Land   12,500

16. Supplies expense $ 100
    Cost of sales   2,000
       Supplies $ 100
       Inventory   2,000

17. Wages $ 80
       Accrued liabilities $ 80
    To accrue for September 27 to
    September 30, wages (This introduces
    the concept of adjustments, covered
    in Chapter 5).

18. Closing entries (to close revenue and expense accounts to retained
    earnings) will be left as an exercise for students (see Problem 3-A
    of this chapter for an example). See if you can arrive at the
    balance for retained earnings.

T-accounts for C3-1:

Cash			
(1)	35,000	10,000	(2)
(11)	5,000	8,000	(4)
(13)	1,000	10,000	(6)
		5,000	(7)
		5,000	(10)
		5,000	(12)
		200	(14)
		2,200	

Accounts receivable – shareholder	
4,000	

Accounts receivable			
(13)	5,000		
(15)	30,000		
	35,000		

Inventory			
(6)	15,000	2,000	(16)
	13,000		

Land			
(1)	50,000	12,500	(15)
	37,500		

Building (net)	
(2)	10,000

Equipment (net)*	
(4)	8,000

Tractor (net)	
(1)	5,000

Incorporation costs*	
(3)	1,000

Supplies			
(5)	10,000	100	(16)
	9,900		

Accounts payable			
(7)	5,000	5,000	(3)
(10)	5,000	10,000	(5)
(12)	5,000	5,000	(6)
		1,500	(8)
		6,500	

Accrued Liabilities			
		80	(17)

Unearned revenue			
		5,000	(11)

Common Shares			
		90,000	(1)

Cost of sales	
(16)	2,000

Sales			
		6,000	(13)

Advertising	
(8)	1,500

Supplies expense	
(16)	100

Gain on sale			
		17,500	(15)

Wages	
(14)	200
(17)	80
	280

Notes: *Separate accounts kept to facilitate income tax objective.

Income Statement for C3-1:

Imperial Soil Limited

Income Statement

Month ended September 30, 19xx

Revenues		
Sales of enriched soil		$ 6,000
Expenses		
Advertising	$1,500	
Wages	280	
Supplies	100	
Cost of enriched soil sold	2,000	3,880
Income before undernoted item		2,120
Gain on sale of excess land**		17,500
Net income***		$19,620

** Notice how this is disclosed separately, as an unusual item.
This draws the reader's attention to a significant non-recurring
event. Later in the course we will discuss these and closely
related events called "extraordinary items."

*** Ignores any income taxes.

Balance Sheet for C3-1:

Imperial Soil Limited

Balance Sheet

September 30, 19xx

Assets

Current assets
Cash in bank* $ (2,200)
Accounts receivable   35,000
Accounts receivable from shareholder   4,000
Inventory of soil   13,000
Supplies   9,900
                                                                  $59,700

Non-current assets
Land $37,500
Building (net)**   10,000
Equipment (net)**   8,000
Tractor (net)**   5,000
Incorporation costs   1,000   61,500

        Total assets $121,200

Liabilities and Shareholder's Equity

Current liabilities
Accounts payable $ 6,500
Accrued liabilities   80
Unearned revenue   5,000
                                                                  $ 11,580

Shareholder's equity
Common shares $90,000
Retained earnings   19,620   109,620

        Total liabilities and shareholder's
        and shareholder's equity $121,200

* The brackets indicate a cash deficit. That is, the company has spent
  more cash than exists in the bank account and we therefore say the
  bank account is in an overdraft position. The company owes the bank
  this amount. Most accountants prefer to show asset accounts such as
  this which are in a net credit balance as a current liability, entitled
  "bank overdraft". This is more correct when amounts are significant.
  The above disclosure may be less confusing for the student at this stage.

** Refers to net of depreciation recorded to date. We did not record any
   depreciation expense for the first month, for simplicity's sake, but in
   practice this would be done, and in future cases it will be done.

- 53 -

4 *Accruing Revenues and Expenses*

The distinction between cash basis and accrual basis accounting, a major theme of Chapter 4, is a most important one, because it recurs throughout the subject and textbooks. Students have to be well prepared to convert cash basis figures to accrual basis, and vice versa. Such knowledge is especially vital for Chapter 14, Statement of Changes in Financial Position, as well as for most succeeding chapters.

The questions in this chapter may prove frustrating at first. Some students may not fully understand the thinking approach which we are using until the course is close to completion, perhaps several weeks from now. Do the best that you can at this point and do not worry if you do not see all of the pieces. Insight will come with practice. Try to think in terms of journal entries.

EXAMPLE 1

The basic cash versus accrual concept can be illustrated as follows:

Accounts receivable – January 1, 19x2 $10,500

All sales are on account. Sales made during January 19x2:

Accounts receivable (asset +) $36,155	
Sales revenue (revenue +)	$36,155

Cash collections of accounts receivable during January 19x2:

Cash (asset +) $38,000	
Accounts receivable (asset –)	$38,000

Required:

Compute the balance in accounts receivable as of January 31, 19x2.

Sales revenue, based on accrual accounting, is $36,155. However, if a cash basis is used, the sales revenue would represent the $38,000 collected on account, because no sales are made for cash.

The question requests a closing balance in accounts receivable, and seemingly is asking for something unrelated to cash versus accrual accounting. The closing balance is:

Accounts receivable, January 1, 19x2 (Debit)	$10,500
Add sales on account (Debit)	36,155
	46,655
Subtract cash collected (Credit)	38,000
Accounts receivable, January 31, 19x2 (Debit)	$ 8,655

However, suppose that we turn the facts around a little and ask another question: how much cash was collected on account? This question involves us in distinuishing cash from accrual accounting.

EXAMPLE 2

Accounts receivable – January 1, 19x2	$10,500
– January 31, 19x2	8,655
All sales are on account; sales in	
January 19x2 amounted to	36,155

Required:

Compute the amount of cash collected on the accounts receivable in January 19x2.

A Solution:

As with Example 1, we are given three items of information and are being asked to compute the fourth item. In Example 2, the fourth item could be called "the cash basis of computing sales," not the accrual basis. The computation is:

Accounts receivable, January 1, 19x2	$10,500
Add sales on account	36,155
	46,655
Subtract the January 31, 19x2 balance	
of accounts receivable	8,655
Amount of cash presumed to be collected	$38,000

In T-account terms, the transactions would be:

Accounts Receivable		
January 1, 19x2 (+) 10,500		
Sales on account (+) 36,155	Cash collections (−) 38,000
January 31, 19x2 (+) 8,655		

We could also ask you to compute the accrual sales revenue figure by providing you with the other three items of information. This is required in Example 3. For practice you might also wish to compute the January 1, 19x2 balance of accounts receivable from the other three items of information.

EXAMPLE 3

Accounts receivable – January 1, 19x2	$10,500
– January 31, 19x2	8,655
Cash collections of accounts receivable during January 19x2	38,000

Required:

Compute the amount of sales on account during January 19x2. (Since in this problem all sales are on account, the question is requesting the accrual sales figure.)

A Solution

Cash collections during January 19x2	$38,000
Add accounts receivable at January 31, 19x2	8,655
	46,655
Subtract accounts receivable at January 1, 19x2	10,500
Sales on account during January 19x2	$36,155

When you feel that you have thoroughly grasped the three examples, you should do case C2-1 in Chapter 2, and then proceed to New Problem 1. in this chapter. As with the previous chapters, try to spend sufficient time on the questions before reading the "Solution" section.

NEW PROBLEM 1 (20-40 minutes)

Compute the cash payments made on accounts payable during 19x3 from the following information:

Inventory – January 1, 19x3 $11,500
          – December 31, 19x3   13,740
Cost of goods (which were) sold in 19x3
                    (expense +)   100,000
Accounts payable – January 1, 19x3   21,815
            – December 31, 19x3   22,990
All purchases were on account; none were
                 made for cash.

Hint: Compute purchases on account from the inventory and cost of goods sold figures; then ascertain the sum needed to balance accounts payable. (Prepare journal entries and post to general ledger T-accounts if you get stuck. No journal entry is needed for the January 1, 19x3 inventory and accounts payable. Just show these sums as opening balances in the respective T-accounts.)

A Solution

We are able to compute the purchases of inventory (goods for resale) for 19x3 using a computation similar to Example 4-3:

Cost of goods which were sold in 19x3 $100,000
Inventory as of December 31, 19x3   13,740
Total inventory available for sale
        during 19x3   113,740
Inventory as of January 1, 19x3   11,500
Goods which must have been purchased
        in 19x3 $102,240

Beginning inventory + purchases = cost of goods sold + ending inventory.

Now that we know the figure for purchases ($102,240), we can put it together with our accounts payable figures and determine the amount of cash paid on the accounts payable. The technique we shall use is similar to Example 2. It involved three debits and one credit in the case of accounts receivable; this problem requires us to look mainly at the credits in order to compute the missing debit to accounts payable.

Accounts payable as of January 1, 19x3 $21,815
Add purchases on account, 19x3 – per our
        computation   102,240
                           124,055
Subtract accounts payable as of
        December 31, 19x3   22,990
Implied cash payment on accounts
        payable $101,065

We arrive at the same figure of $101,065 by preparing journal entries and posting them to ledger T-accounts:

1. Accounts payable, January 1, 19x3: (No journal entry required in 19x3 because the goods were purchased in 19x2)

2. Purchases in 19x3:

    Inventory (or purchases) $102,240
      Accounts payable $102,240

3. Cash payments on accounts payable in 19x3:

    Accounts payable $101,065
      Cash $101,065

Although we normally would post all debits and credits, we need post only those affecting accounts payable to prove the foregoing.

	Accounts Payable	
	January 1, 19x3 (+)	21,815
	Purchases (+)	102,240
Cash payments (−) $101,065		
	December 31, 19x3 (+)	22,990

Similarly we can prove our figure of $102,240 for purchases by recording the entires affecting the inventory account:

1. Inventory, January 1, 19x3: (No journal entry required in 19x3 because the goods were purchased in 19x2)

2. Purchases in 19x3: (This is just a repeat of journal entry 2. given earlier)

    Inventory (or purchases) $102,240
      Accounts payable $102,240

3. Cost of goods sold in 19x3:

    Cost of goods sold (expense +) $100,000
      Inventory (asset −) $100,000

	Inventory	
January 1, 19x3 (+) 11,500		
Purchases (+) 102,240		
	Goods sold (−) 100,000	
December 31, 19x3 13,740		

This problem should not be attempted until Appendix 4-A in the textbook has been read. The textbook recommends that Appendix 4-A be read only after the concepts in Chapter 4 have been grasped.

Prepare *adjusting* journal entries at December 31, 19x1, for each of the following unrelated situations. Assumptions are required and should be clearly stated.

1. A 12-month insurance policy commencing December 1, 19x1, was purchased for $3,600 and paid for in cash in early December.

2. $15,000 in cash was received from a customer on December 10, 19x1, for goods to be delivered when completed. Unfortunately, the goods were not completed and shipped until January 19x2.

3. A fixed asset costing $12,000 and having a life of 10 years was purchased December 1, 19x1, and charged to cost of goods sold.

4. On December 6, 19x1, wages for November 19x1 were paid and wage expense was debited for $3,456.

5. Another company paid us $6,000 on December 15, 19x1, for use of a portion of our building until March 15, 19x2.

A Solution

This question cannot be solved unless we make several assumptions about what happened earlier in the recording process. We are being asked for adjusting journal entries and can make these only when we know the original transaction journal entries, which were made and posted to ledger accounts. Before we make any adjusting journal entry we must ask ourselves:

First - How much debit or credit *is* currently recorded in the unadjusted ledger accounts?

Second - How much *should be* recorded in the ledger account after adjustment?

Third - How much debit or credit must be recorded to adjust from "what is" to "what should be"?

Fourth - What other account is similarly affected? (Remember, adjusting journal entries usually do not affect cash.)

1. Let us select transaction 1. to illustrate the foregoing. There are at least three different adjusting journal entries which could be provided, depending upon which of three original transaction journal entries was made. After adjustment, we want the following amounts in

each ledger account:

Prepaid insurance: 11/12 x $3,600 = <u>$3,300</u>

Insurance expense: 1/12 x $3,600 = <u>$ 300</u>

If original transaction journal entry on December 1 was:	Then the adjusting journal entry on December 31, would be:

a. Prepaid insurance $3,600
   Cash $3,600
	a. Insurance expense $ 300
	   Prepaid insurance $ 300

b. Insurance expense $3,600
   Cash $3,600
	b. Prepaid insurance $3,300
	   Insurance expense $3,300

c. Prepaid insurance $3,300
   Insurance expense   300
   Cash $3,600
	c. No adjusting entry required

Hence, we have to make an assumption about which of a., b., or c. was recorded as our original transaction journal entry before we can give adjusting journal entry.

This type of less directed question tells the instructor how well a student understands adjusting journal entries and the accrual versus cash basis of accounting. Students who have memorized instead of having understood tend to provide adjusting entry a. regardless of the facts.

A similar approach is used in solving 2. to 5.:

2.

If original transaction journal entry on December 10 was:	Then the adjusting journal entry on December 31 would be:
a. Cash $15,000 Unearned revenue $15,000	a. No adjusting entry required

b. Cash $15,000
   Revenue $15,000
	b. Revenue $15,000
	   Unearned revenue $15,000

After the adjusting journal entries have been posted we will show $15,000 of unearned revenue and zero revenue. This is what we desire -- assuming that revenue is not recorded until goods are shipped. Chapter 5 has more to say on this topic, however.

3. This transaction has two levels of concern because fixed assets depreciate. The initial adjusting or correcting journal entry is:

Fixed asset $12,000
   Cost of goods sold $12,000

When this entry is posted, both the balance sheet account for fixed assets and the income statement account for cost of goods (which were) sold are as they should be, except for recording depreciation on the fixed asset. If we assume straight line depreciation, our second adjusting entry is:

Depreciation expense	$ 100	
Accumulated depreciation		$ 100
To record expiry of 1/120 of the asset's life.		

4. This transaction is trickier than the others because we have to make a different type of assumption. *If* the company closes its books annually on December 31, then there is nothing wrong with the original transaction journal entry. Hence, no adjusting journal entry is required.

However, *if* the company closed its books on November 30, 19x1, it would have (we assume) made the following adjusting journal entry at that date:

Wage expense	$3,456	
Accrued wages payable		$3,456

This means that after the December 6, 19x1 and November 30, 19x1 journal entries are posted, the two affected ledger accounts would show, on December 31, 19x1, before adjustment:

Accrued wages payable (nor November)	$3,456 Credit
Wage expense	$3,456 Debit

Since both of these accounts and sums pertain to November, we would have to make the following correcting or adjusting (sometimes it is also called "reversing") journal entry to reduce the balances to zero:

Accrued wages payable	$3,456	
Wages expense		$3,456

Once this entry is posted we can concentrate our efforts on seeing whether an accrual is needed for December wages. (The question is silent on the December 31 accrual.)

5. This situation is the opposite of the transaction in 1. As of December 31, 19x1, after any adjustment, we want $5,000 in an unearned revenue account and $1,000 in a revenue account. Our adjusting journal entry depends on the original transaction entry

which was made:

If original transaction journal entry on December 15 was:	Then the adjusting journal entry on December 31 would be:

a. Cash $6,000
   Unearned income $5,000
   revenue   1,000
	a. None required

b. Cash $6,000
   Unearned revenue $6,000
	b. Unearned revenue $1,000
	   Revenue $1,000

c. Cash $6,000
   Revenue $6,000
	c. Revenue $5,000
	   Unearned revenue $5,000

If you experience difficulty in following this type of question, try posting the journal entries to the ledger accounts. This better enables you to see what is happening and observe that the closing balance in the accounts are those which you wish to see. One other aid would be to prepare a list of accounts which "go together." This list will help you avoid needless grouping and incorrect debits or credits to cash. A partial list is:

Income statement account	Offsetting balance sheet account
a. Revenue	a. Unearned revenue or revenue received in advance
b. Expense	b. Accrued (expense) payable; or Prepaid expense
c. Depreciation expense	c. Accumulated depreciation

TEXTBOOK *C4-2: A SOLUTION (60-90 minutes)

The textbook should be referred to for the Good Boy Limited question; here is a response. Some students may wish to postpone this question until they have read Chapter 5; parts b. and c. are difficult.

This question is labelled as a case because parts b. and c. require considerable thought after the basic bookkeeping journal entries have been compiled and posted. Some of the material has already been covered in the textbook and in this manual, but other parts require some imagination and forward thinking about the purposes and uses of accounting. A good response to parts b. and c. requires considerable practice, and your "answer" is not likely to include much of what is provided hereunder.

Rather than respond to the question in the order indicated under the textbook "required," let us provide some background or context so as to enable greater appreciation of the financial statements. The reasons for providing the context will be clearer after you have read Chapter 5 of the textbook. You also are advised to refer to this question after

you have read Chapters 6 or 7 of the textbook, because you will see
more in the response than you will appreciate at the Chapter 4 stage of
the course.

Some objectives, or purposes, or reasons, for accounting and preparing
financial statements for GBL are:

1. To portray solvency for the benefit of present creditors. Notes
    payable are coming due in four months; yet the company at August 31,
    19x7 has a negative working capital position.

2. To secure additional capital or credit for expansion. Hence, cash
    flow prediction is important, because lenders wish to know how and
    when they will be repaid. (See Chapter 5.)

3. Performance appraisal of each retail appliance store manager is
    needed. Hence, disclosure of income for each store would help poten-
    tial investors.

4. The decision of Mr. T. Oaster to retire. How well is the company
    doing? How much could he realize by selling out now? How much will
    he realize by staying in for three more years? This involves the
    prediction objective, noted in 2. above.

The above are ranked in order of importance. Less important in this case
are internal control (no apparent problem exists in this respect), income
taxation (the issues at hand do not significantly affect measurement of
taxable income), stewardship (we have an owner/manager situation, and there
is no suggestion in the case that the present creditor requires audited
financial statements.)

As a result of the above purposes, particular accounting issues take on
greater significance than would be the situation with a stable company
with fewer problems and moderate owner aspirations. The specific accounting and related problems are:

1. Valuation of receivables and inventory. Given the potential solvency
    problem and the prediction objective, readers probably are *very*
    interested in amounts which will be realized in the coming period
    from current assets. Hence, decisions on a bad debt allowance and
    a provision for inventory obsolescence (no information given) are
    critical.

2. There is missing information regarding depreciation. An assumption
    is required about previous depreciation rates and any expense to
    date hidden in cost of goods sold. (See Appendices 4-B and 4-C.)

3. Is there a going-concern problem? (Will the company go bankrupt?)
    Will the company be able to secure enough cash to repay the note
    plus interest in four months? Given this, will fixed asset costs
    be recovered?

4. How well is *each* store doing?

5. Given the cash bind and the need to secure additional financing, current replacement costs (or some other appraised value) of property, plant, and equipment should be estimated. (See prediction objective above. Lenders want to know the amount of security for any loan which they make.)

6. The creditor must decide on the amount of any loan to the company.

7. Potential investors must decide whether to invest in the company.

8. Mr. Oaster must decide what to do.

The above problems are not ranked, since they are of roughly equal importance. Let us elaborate on the above eight problems:

1. Later chapters in the textbook discuss legal constraints and the possible constraint of generally accepted accounting principles. Constraints confine or restrict us in our choice of accounting principles and disclosure. They may prevent us from tailoring our financial statements to particular users. A small one-owner company such as GBL is not likely to have to be concerned about legal constraints, which generally apply to larger size companies which have sold shares or bonds to the general public. If Mr. Oaster does not have to have his financial statements audited (by a CA, for example) to satisfy creditors, then he may also be free of the constraint of generally accepted accounting principles as set forth in the *CICA Handbook*. Mr. Oaster could request a "special purpose" accounting report (which need not be in accordance with GAAP) instead of a general purpose report.

   The special purpose report could then attempt, moreso than one based on historic cost, to aid in prediction of the (future) cash receipts less disbursements of GBL. The controller will have to persuade Mr. Oaster that the *objectives* outlined above (especially prediction) are best facilitated by writing receivables and inventory down to realizable values. Separate disclosure of the write-downs or contras to receivables and inventory will help readers decide whether the provisions are sufficient.

   Existing and potential creditors may also require special purpose aging analyses of inventory and receivables. (see Chapters 7 to 9.)

2. An assumption is required. It is plausible that past entries have been ($6,000/6) $1,000 a year straight-line depreciation.

3. There is no going-concern problem, provided Mr. Oaster can secure additional financing to replace the debt. But does Mr. Oaster want to be held personally liable for any new debt? A personal guarantee on his house and car and furniture will likely be required. Is the risk he faces tolerable? See 8. below — Mr. Oaster may want to sell

out at this point, and leave new capital infusion and assumption of risks to new owners.

4. This is primarily a management issue. However, external readers (especially investors) will be interested in any of what is called "segmented data" (sales, gross profits, and income by store) in the financial statements.

5. The controller can estimate current replacement costs, perhaps with the help of a qualified appraiser. These should be disclosed in the annual statements, probably in a footnote.

6. Given the present working capital (current assets minus current liabilities) deficit and the note coming due, a creditor would *not* likely want to loan new money unless there was a further infusion of equity (share) capital. The cyclical nature of the company's business adds further risk. The creditors would want additional information, such as the age of accounts receivable and inventory, cash flow forecasts, current values of fixed assets, and possibly a Statement of Changes in Financial Position (SCFP). They would likely want the personal guarantee of owners, and request "mortgages" on personal assets of Mr. and Mrs. Oaster.

7. The potential investor is interested in growth prospects in earnings and share value. Past trends are of interest for this purpose. The book return on shareholder's equity (net income divided by common shares and retained earnings) is presently $10,575/$95,575, or around 9%.

The investor must also consider:

a. the cyclical nature of this business. (Hence, past and forecast data for this industry would be useful);

b. the performance by each store; should one store be closed if it is not successful?

8. Mr. Oaster wants to retire in three years. The decision he faces is to sell now or in three years. It is unlikely that he will be able to finance replacement of debt (let alone the planned growth) without substantial common share infusion (selling shares to others). This would reduce his interest in net income for the next three years. Further, personal guarantees on any new debt will expose him to substantial risk given his age. Students can estimate his likely return on investment over the next three years (adjusting for his salary and any income dilution) *compared to* interest at, say, 12% on the proceeds from selling the company. The best bet would appear to be to sell now.

Various recommendations might be made, such as the following:

1. Write receivables and inventory down to net realizable or cash values

and disclose the amount of allowances for write-downs for creditors who want to predict cash receipts and disbursements of the future years.

2. Record depreciation for 19x7 on a straight-line basis, provided this approximates wear and tear. Potential investors want income trends.

3. It is premature to conclude that the going-concern basis of accounting is no longer appropriate. GBL is not about to go bankrupt.

4. Disclose sales and costs by store in external statements for potential investors who want to predict.

5. Disclose replacement costs of fixed assets in a note to external statements, for creditors and potential investors.

6.
to Mr. Oaster might wish to sell his interest in the company now, provided
8. a reasonable price can be secured. An alternative is to sell only a portion. Further credit is unlikely to be granted to him until more common share capital is injected into the company.

The financial statements and adjusting entries needed to prepare them are:

Adjusting Journal Entries

1. Bad debt expense $12,000
       Allowance for doubtful accounts $12,000

2. Insurance expense (Office expenses) $ 3,600
       Unexpired insurance $ 3,600

3. Salaries expense $ 1,500
       Accrued liabilities $ 1,500

4. Interest expense $ 4,000
       Accrued interest payable $ 4,000

5. Heat, light and power expense $ 800
       Accrued liabilities $ 800

6. Cost of goods sold $15,000
       Inventory $15,000

7. Depreciation expense $10,000
       Accumulated depreciation $10,000

   An assumption is required here.
   Straight line looks plausible.

8. Income tax expense $ 3,525
       Income tax payable $ 3,525

The company probably enjoys the low rate of tax (25%). However, up to a 50% rate would be an acceptable alternative assumption.

Good Boy Limited
Income Statement
Year ended August 31, 19x7

Sales		$510,000
Cost of goods sold		255,000
Gross margin		255,000
Operating expenses:		
Salaries	$81,500	
Office expenses	35,600	
Heat, light and power	10,800	
Selling expense	75,000	
Bad debt expense	12,000	
Depreciation expense	10,000	224,900
Income from operations		30,100
Interest expense		16,000
Income before income taxes		14,100
Income taxes		3,525
Net income		$ 10,575

Good Boy Limited
Balance Sheet
August 31, 19x7

Assets			Liabilities		
Current assets:			Current liabilities:		
Cash		$ 1,000	Accounts payable		$150,000
Accounts receivable	$150,000		Accrued liabilities		2,300
Less allowance for			Notes payable		200,000
doubtful accounts	12,000	138,000	Interest payable		4,000
Inventory		185,000	Income taxes payable		3,525
Prepaid insurance		1,400			
Total current assets		325,400	Total current liabilities		359,825
Fixed assets:			Shareholder's equity		
Property, plant and			Common shares		30,000
equipment	200,000		Retained earnings		65,575
Less accumulated					95,575
depreciation	70,000				
Total fixed assets		130,000	Total liabilities and shareholder's equity		$455,400
Total assets		$455,400			

5

Revenues and Expenses

In Chapter 3, while discussing C3-1, we looked at the objectives of accounting information. The list presented there (long run earnings and cash flow prediction objective, short run liquidity assessment objective, the stewardship objective, the performance appraisal objective, the internal control objective, the income tax objective, and the compliance objective) is very similar to the list of objectives or reasons for accounting appearing in Chapter 5 of the text. Differences between the lists are a matter of form, not of substance. The first problem discussed in this chapter, Textbook *P5-1, examines how the objectives of accounting information might differ between a large public company engaged in steel manufacturing and a local men's clothing store.

TEXTBOOK *P5-1: A SOLUTION (25-40 minutes)

The discussion might take the following form:

Large Public Steel Company

1. There is separation of owners and management. If the steel company's shares are widely held, shareholders will not have much knowledge of the daily operating affairs of the business. These shareholders will typically rely heavily on the financial statements to gain desired information. Among other things, shareholders will want to assess whether, overall, management has taken actions in the best interests of shareholders. Accordingly, stewardship and evaluation of management performance are important objectives for accounting information.

    A stewardship accounting report tells the lender or investor of funds what management has done with those funds. Much of the requirements of securities legislation, the Canada Business Corporations Act, and the *CICA Handbook* are geared to the stewardship objective of reporting. That is, these "stewardship" requirements protect the shareholder by prescribing a minimum amount of financial statement reporting. For the large publicly-owned company, compliance with these "stewardship" requirements is very important.

Financial statements also tell shareholders and lenders, in broad terms, how management has performed with the funds loaned or invested (the evaluation of performance objective). For our steel company, shareholders may look to earnings or earnings per share or some other measure of performance, to tell them (simply and quickly) how the company performed for the year. This explains why the management of a large public steel company might be very concerned about published earnings figures. This sets the stage for potential conflict with auditors over issues like revenue and expense recognition, write-downs of assets, and so on. Students should be alert to detect instances where the performance appraisal objective is motivating a particular (perhaps questionable) accounting treatment or disclosure proposed by management.

In summary, suffice it to say that stewardship and evaluation of management performance are two important objectives for a large public company.

2. Shareholders typically want information to facilitate their decision to buy, sell or hold shares. This has been referred to in the text as the prediction objective. For a large public steel company, shareholders will look to financial statements as one source of information about the future prospects (growth in earnings, future dividend payouts, and so on) of the company. Hence, accountants will want to be alert to this prediction objective when preparing statements, perhaps in deciding when to recognize revenue on the sale of steel or in deciding to disclose information in a note pertaining to the shutdown of a steel mill. In the former instance, shareholders would prefer to know about a sale as soon as possible, if the information is "reasonably" reliable. Perhaps recognition of revenue on completion of production is justified for steel manufactured to order for reliable buyers. Students should notice that this would not violate any of the four tests of revenue recognition outlined in Chapter 5 of the text. In the latter instance, shareholders want to know on a timely basis about important event, like a shutdown, which will affect future earnings.

3. Possibly, the steel company needs access to large credit markets (or sources of cash funds). Hence, financial statements must help portray short run and long run liquidity. Creditors will want to assess the ability of the company to repay loan principal and interest, as well as to meet other cash obligations. They will look carefully at the balance sheet, to assess working capital (current assets minus current liabilities) and perhaps to assess the security underlying their loan. (Can the assets be sold at prices which will be high enough to repay the loan?) They will probably also look to the statement of changes in financial position, to see where liquid funds came from and where they went to. (This is discussed in Chapter 14.) Students should note that, in our revenue recognition example above, creditors may not care about early revenue recognition, provided the resulting accounts receivable represents a reasonably reliable asset.

4. The large public steel company may also want to minimize the payment of income taxes. However, because we have assumed that it needs regular access to capital or credit markets, the above three objectives of accounting are more important than this objective.

   For example, the steel company would not want to delay recognition of revenue (to, say, recognition upon collection of cash) so as to defer income tax payments, given its prediction objective. Such a delay would withhold information on sales until they are collected in cash -- which would be too late for those who want to estimate future success.

5. For the steel company, internal accounting control is important but is probably well looked after by a competent accounting staff and therefore is not a problem which we need be concerned about.

Men's Clothing Store

1. The company is owner-managed. Hence, the stewardship and management evaluation objectives are less important. (The manager does not need a report for himself about his own activities.) Hence, compliance with the "stewardship" requirements of GAAP, Companies Acts, and securities legislation are probably less important. Why is this so? Recall that, for the steel company, investors bought shares and in return were entitled to a minimum amount of information from the company about how the investment was doing. Here, the owner and manager are the same person. There is no duty to report from the latter to the former. The clothing store may not even require a "statutory" audit. A "statutory" audit is one for the benefit of shareholders, usually prescribed by companies law for companies over a certain size or for companies with more than a few shareholders. The clothing store is unlike the public steel company which almost certainly requires a statutory audit.

2. Provided ownership is likely to remain in the same hands and a banker does not want a financial statement for prediction purposes, the prediction of future prospects of the clothing store may not be an important objective of the clothing store. Contrast this with the large public steel company which has to borrow money from the public at frequent intervals. For this reason (e.g., because prediction is less important), the clothing store might choose to delay its revenue recognition point (say, to the point of cash collection from customers). This may conform with "generally accepted accounting principles" because individual customers may be less reliable and the sale may not be assured until cash is collected. Such a delay would cater to the income tax objective of accounting, which allows the postponement of income tax payments, an important objective, as we shall see next.

3. Tax minimization may be an important objective (especially if cash is scarce). In the example above, generally accepted accounting principles would allow revenue recognition to the point of completion

of production of a custom-made suit. Recall the four tests of revenue
recognition outlined in Chapter 5 of the text. A sale is secured,
provided the order is non-cancellable and cash collection is assured.
Revenue can then be objectively measured. The major portion of costs
has been incurred at completion of production. If the customer is new,
some credit check could be performed and some allowance for an uncollectible portion of the amount owing (bad debt) could be made. In
summary, the facts would allow revenue recognition upon completion of
production.

Yet, because tax minimization is probably important to the owner,
recognition upon cash receipt may be chosen to delay income recognition as long as possible, an alternative that "GAAP" would probably
also permit (due to uncertainty about cash collection). Who is
going to challenge such a treatment, especially if there is some
risk and uncertainty about collection of cash? The owner? Certainly
not. Income tax officials? Possibly. A banker or creditor? Maybe
and maybe not. Let us look at their needs next.

4. Creditors of the clothing store will tend to consist of the bank and
    a few suppliers. The information requirements of these creditors will
    tend to be simple, and *may* be fulfilled by special purpose reports.
    These include cash budgets, and other statements which are discussed
    in later accounting courses. The creditors will look to financial
    statements for some assurance as to the cash liquidity (ability to
    meet cash obligations in the near future) of the company. They may
    not care very much about when a sale is recognized. Even if the
    creditor requires that there be an audit of the financial statements,
    the auditor is not likely to challenge the delay in revenue recogni-
    tion as not being in accordance with GAAP.

    What is the lesson here? It is that the "facts" will often allow more
    than one acceptable "GAAP" treatment. Hence, the accountant or the
    reader of statements must look carefully at the possible objectives
    guiding the preparation of statements. In this case, the tax mini-
    mization objective may be of greatest importance, and with unclear
    facts and uncertainty, the result could be delayed revenue recogni-
    tion.

5. Internal control may be an important objective for the clothing store.
    The accounting staff is likely to be small, and it is therefore diffi-
    cult to segregate duties and thereby help prevent fraud and error.
    Hence, the record-keeping system will have to be carefully designed
    so as to provide a complete trail of transactions which in turn will
    minimize the chances of fraud.

Perspective

Notice how, in P5-1, we used revenue recognition to illustrate how the
selection of accounting principles must be tailored to suit the objectives
of accounting information, which will differ from company to company. We
will explore this theme in more depth in New Problem 1., following, deal-
ing with revenue recognition.

NEW PROBLEM 1 (60-80 minutes)

Required:

a. Prepare journal entires to record revenues and expenses as well as
    assets and liabilities to conform with the basis of revenue recogni-
    tion indicated in each of the following situations:

    i. ABC Ltd., in 19x1, purchases for $25,000, on account, equipment
    intended for resale. In 19x2, the company pays the $25,000 owed to
    the supplier. In the same year, it sells the equipment for $40,000
    cash, and gives the customer a one-year warranty against defects.
    The company's best guess is that its cost of making repairs under
    the warranty will be $1,000. In 19x3, the company incurs $900 in
    repair costs prior to expiration of the warranty. ABC Ltd. recog-
    nizes revenue at the time of sale.

    ii. DEF Ltd., in 19x1, contracts with the local government to build
    an Olympic ski jump at a price of $50 million for a certain county
    sponsoring the 19x2 winter Olympics. DEF Ltd. estimates that total
    construction costs will be $40 million. However, actual final costs
    in excess of estimates are common for such projects. In 19x1, it
    begins construction and incurs $15 million in costs. In 19x2, it
    incurs $27 million in costs and completes the project. In 19x3, the
    company collects the full contract price from the government. DEF
    Ltd. recognizes revenue on a completed contract basis.

    iii. GHI Ltd., a gold mining company, discovers ore which will
    produce 1,000 ounces of gold in 19x1, and spends $20,000 to process
    that ore into a finished stage. GHI Ltd. has a firm contract sell-
    ing price of $500 an ounce (slightly below the world market price)
    with reliable customers. In 19x2, customers pick up gold from
    GHI Ltd. (delivery costs are zero) and pay cash upon pick-up.
    GHI Ltd. recognizes revenue at completion of ore processing (when the
    gold is in its finished goods form).

    iv. In 19x1, JKL Ltd. opens a business in order to sell appliances.
    The company is forced by competitive conditions to give generous
    credit terms. One year is allowed before payment is due; finance
    charges are 20 percent per annum. The economy is in recession, and
    customers are sometimes unable to pay what they owe to JKL Ltd.
    In 19x1, JKL sells to a customer, for $1,000, an appliance purchased
    some time ago at a cost of $500. In 19x2, that customer pays the
    entire amount owed, including finance charges of $200. JKL Ltd.
    recognizes interest and sales revenue as cash is collected.

    v. In 19x1, MNO Ltd., an established seller of office equipment,
    sells equipment (which originally cost the company $300) to a
    customer for $500, on account. The customer has three months to
    pay. Following a credit check, MNO Ltd.'s best guess is that there
    is a small chance that the customer will be unable to pay in three
    months time. Accordingly, MNO Ltd. decides to make an allowance for

bad debts (that is, an allowance for the uncollectible portion of accounts receivable) of $50. MNO Ltd. recognizes revenue at the time of sale.

b. For each of the five situations above, explain why the chosen basis of revenue recognition makes sense (that is, fits the facts and possible objectives of accounting) given the following additional information about each company:

i. ABC Ltd. is owner-managed, with no creditors other than the supplier.

ii. The shares of DEF Ltd. are widely-held and actively traded. The company has a bank loan outstanding which will be paid out of the excess of contract revenue over contract costs once DEF Ltd. is paid by the government.

iii. The shares of GHI Ltd. are widely-held and actively traded, and there are no major creditors. However, a bonus is paid to management based on net income.

iv. JKL Ltd. is owner-managed, and because cash is scarce, seeks to delay the payment of income taxes as long as possible. The company has a bank loan outstanding which is secured by the accounts receivable of JKL Ltd.

v. MNO Ltd. is owner-managed, and the owner wants to sell his business any time during the next three years. Sales are increasing rapidly each year. The company has plenty of cash and no creditors.

A *Solution*

a. Required Journal Entries:

i. ABC Ltd.   19x1

1.

Merchandise inventory (asset +)	$25,000	
Accounts payable (liability +)		$25,000

To record the purchase of inventory, on account.

19x2

2.

Accounts payable (liability -)	$25,000	
Cash (asset -)		$25,000

To record payment to supplier.

3.

Cash (asset +) $40,000
  Sales revenue (revenue +) $40,000
To record the sale of the equipment.

4.

Cost of goods sold (expense +) $25,000
Warranty expense (expense +)   1,000
  Merchandise inventory (asset −) $25,000
  Warranty liability (liability +)   1,000
To recognize expenses associated with the revenue
recognized.

Students should note that warranty liability represents an estimate of
costs to be incurred in the future. Such costs are recognized in the
same accounting period that associated revenues are recognized, in
order to ensure that costs are "matched" with revenues (the matching
concept).

19x3

5.

Warranty liability (liability −) $ 1,000
  Cash (asset −) $ 900
  Warranty expense (expense −)   100
To record costs incurred to fulfill the warranty
obligation.

The estimate for warranty costs in 19x2 turned out to be overstated by
$100. To be correct, the warranty liability account should have a zero
balance at the end of 19x3 (assuming no other warranty transactions
exist), since there is no further obligation. Hence, we recognize the
$100 "error" in estimate as a reduction in expense in 19x3. (In situa-
tions where we have to make estimates, using the best information
available, prior years' expenses are not restated.) The $100 is prob-
ably a tolerable error in estimate, as far as users are concerned.
Certainly, they would rather have the company's best estimate in 19x2
(possibly for prediction purposes, for stewardship, etc.), provided
errors in estimate are "tolerably" low.

ii. <u>DEF Ltd.</u>   19x1

1.

Construction in progress, at cost (asset +) $15,000,000
  Cash (asset −) $15,000,000
To record costs incurred in construction of
the ski jump.

2.

Construction in progress, at cost (asset +)	$27,000,000	
Cash (asset –)		$27,000,000

To record costs incurred in construction of
the ski jump.

3.

Accounts receivable (asset +)	$50,000,000	
Revenue (revenue +)		$50,000,000

To recognize revenue on completion of
construction.

4.

Cost of construction (expense +)	$42,000,000	
Construction in progress, at cost (asset –)		$42,000,000

To record expenses incurred in earning the
construction revenue.

Students should carefully compare the completed contract method used
here to the percentage of completion method illustrated in Chapter 5
of the text. Here, no revenue is recognized until the contract terms
are fulfilled, which we assume takes place when construction is complete. Had the question told us that the government has the right
under the contract to withhold approval for, say, six months while
inspection takes place, then revenue could be recognized after the
six months elapses and the contract is fulfilled. Under this method
we do not wait another year, until the government pays, to recognize
revenue because 1) cash collection is almost certain; 2) all costs
and revenues are known; and 3) the sale is final upon completion of
the contract. (Recall the four guidelines or "tests" of revenue
recognition under the stewardship objective, outlined in Chapter 5.)
We do not recognize revenue prior to contract completion because
costs are uncertain until the project is complete.

19x3

5.

Cash (asset +)	$50,000,000	
Accounts receivable (asset +)		$50,000,000

To record payment of the contract price by
the government.

iii. <u>GHI Ltd</u>.   19x1

During Processing of Ore

1.

Work in process (asset +)	$ 20,000	
Cash (asset –)		$ 20,000

To record costs of processing the discovered
gold ore.

At Completion of Processing

2.

Finished gold, at cost (asset +) $ 20,000
  Work in process (asset -) $ 20,000
To record completion of ore processing.

3.

Finished gold, at selling price (asset +) $500,000
  Manufacturing revenue (revenue +) $500,000
To recognize revenue upon completion of ore
processing.

Students should note that inventories are, in effect, carried at selling price rather than at cost. This is because we recognize revenue
while the ore is still in the company's inventory. This meets the
four stewardship guidelines for revenue recognition because, at the
completion of processing, revenue is assured. A buyer can always be
found, possibly at a selling price in excess of contract price, if
some contract buyer defaults on the purchase; costs are known; the
production is complete; and cash collection is assured.

19x2

At Time of Pick Up

4.

Cash (asset +) $500,000
  Finished gold, at selling price (asset -) $500,000
To record the pick up of gold ore by customers.

Students should observe that no revenue is recognized in 19x2. Also,
had there been delivery costs, these (estimated costs) would have been
accrued in 19x1 to reflect the expense in the period in which the
revenue is recognized. This is in accordance with the matching concept.

iv. <u>JKL Ltd.</u>   19x2

1.

Cash (asset +) $ 1,200
  Sales revenue (revenue +) $ 1,000
  Interest revenue (revenue +)   200
To record revenue upon collection of cash.

2.

Cost of goods sold (expense +) $ 500
  Merchandise inventory (asset -) $ 500
To record the expenses associated with the
revenue recognized.

Students should note that no entries are required for 19x1, even though delivery took place in 19x1. This is because revenues and related expenses are recognized in 19x2. Recognition in 19x1 upon delivery would not have met our four stewardship guidelines for revenue recognition because eventual collection of cash would not be reasonably assured and a substantial portion of sales effort consists of collecting the cash.

v. MNO Ltd.   19x1

1.

Accounts receivable (asset +)	$500	
Sales revenue (revenue +)		$500

To record the sale of office equipment.

2.

Cost of goods sold (expense +)	$300	
Bad debt expense (expense +)	50	
Merchandise inventory (asset −)		$300
Allowance for bad debts (asset contra +)		50

To record the expenses associated with the revenue recognized.

The concept of bad debt allowances is not covered until a later chapter, so students may want to come back to this entry at a later stage if it is not understood. The $50 represents an estimate of the uncollectible portion of the account receivable. Accountants refer to it as an expense, by convention, rather than a reduction of revenues. The associated credit entry is to a contra account which is netted against accounts receivable, much like accumulated depreciation is netted against the asset. The important point to note at this stage is that MNO recognizes revenue in 19x1 (upon sale), even though cash collection is uncertain. (This seems to violate one of our four revenue recognition tests.) It is able to do this because some "reasonable" estimate of the uncollectible portion can be made. Hence, we can say that cash collection is "reasonably" certain, and regard our fourth test for revenue recognition as being met, after we record the estimate for uncollected cash in our "bad debt expense" and "allowance for bad debts" account. It is very common for companies to make such estimates rather than delay the recognition of revenue, especially where the companies have users who want to predict (our prediction objective). Once again, as in warranty expense, we tolerate some loss in objectivity by making estimates so that the resulting figures can be more relevant for users, especially users who want to predict earnings on a timely basis.

b. Logic

i. ABC Ltd. is owner-managed, with no creditors other than suppliers. Therefore, its probable objectives of accounting information are income tax minimization and internal control. Students may wonder why we did not defer recognition until, say, the expiry of the warranty period, when all costs are known for certain. This is a matter of judgment. Costs (the warranty expense, in particular) are "reasonably" capable of estimation in 19x1. All other revenue recognition tests for stewardship are met. Hence, the Income Tax officials would not likely accept a delay of revenue recognition. Recall that, on several previous occasions, we have emphasized that the Income Tax Act often looks to generally accepted accounting principles for guidance on income measurement for income tax purposes. This is one such instance.

Finally, the internal control objective is probably not affected much by the timing of revenue recognition. This is provided that ABC Ltd. has good records to keep track of shipments, who owes what to whom, and so on. Having the receivable in the general ledger sooner as opposed to later probably does not add much to control.

ii. DEF Ltd. is a widely-held company with debt to be repaid out of what is left over after costs have been paid and cash is collected from the government. Therefore, its probable objectives are: 1) information to facilitate stewardship reporting; 2) information to facilitate the loan decision by creditors; and 3) information to help shareholders predict future earnings prospects.

Why does delayed revenue recognition (completed contract) make sense? Here, we have a conflict between objectives. Shareholders who want to predict lose out because they do not see the revenue and corresponding income from the project until completion. Note disclosure of expenses and contract prices in the financial statements might help this group, especially if investors are reasonably quick to grasp this sort of information disclosed in notes (the efficient capital markets issue).

Creditors probably are better off by delay of revenue recognition. Why? Loan decisions just might be based on financial accounting data, particularly the excess of project revenue over project cost. It might be best to wait until these figures are reasonably "objective" and reliable, due to the possibility of cost overruns. For the same reason (need for "objective" figures), the stewardship objective of reporting is probably better served by delay of recognition. Recall one of the four stewardship tests of revenue recognition which says that recognition should be delayed until costs are reasonably certain.

iii. GHI Ltd. is widely-held, there are no major creditors, and a bonus is based on net income. The objectives of accounting for GHI Ltd. are: 1) information to facilitate stewardship reporting; 2) information to facilitate performance appraisal of management by shareholders (that is, does a large bonus reflect good performance, or has there been a manipulation of net income figures?); and 3) information to facilitate prediction by shareholders. Why does revenue recognition at completion of ore processing make sense?

Clearly, shareholders who want to predict are benefited from timely disclosure of earnings. (Earnings trends are pointed out earlier.) Stewardship does not suffer, since our four tests of revenue recognition are met (see part a. above). Does performance appraisal suffer? Probably not. Income computation at completion of processing probably provides a sufficiently objective and unbiased measure of "good or bad performance," since the ore is "as good as sold" at this point and all costs are known or estimable with little error.

iv. JKL Ltd. is owner-managed, and has a bank loan secured by accounts receivable. Its probable objectives are: 1) stewardship reporting to the bank; 2) information to facilitate the bank's loan decision; and 3) income tax minimization. Does a cash basis of revenue recognition make sense? As discussed in part a., the stewardship tests of revenue recognition are best met in this situation with uncertain collection by delay of recognition until cash is collected. The banker's needs are also probably better served by delay, since he might otherwise base the loan decision on an accounts receivable figure that is not very reliable. What about income tax? The delay probably helps defer income tax payments. For JKL Ltd., all objectives might be best served by delay.

v. MNO Ltd. is owner-managed, there are no creditors, income tax delay does not seem overly important, and the owner wants to sell the business. Therefore, the main objective of accounting is probably prediction of earnings and long-term cash flow by prospective buyers of the business. In this light, recognition of revenue upon sale with a reasonable allowance for bad debts makes sense, especially since sales are growing. This is more timely recognition than if we had waited until cash collection to recognize revenue, as we did for JKL Ltd. A needless delay of revenue recognition might hurt the seller, and benefit the buyer, if a sales price for the company's shares is based on recorded earnings. Both seller and buyer probably have some tolerance for "reasonable" errors in estimates of the proportion of receivables which are likely to be uncollectible.

Let us now try a case which requires an application of the Key Concepts in Chapter 5. You might want to review these in the textbook before attempting a response. The Appendix to Chapter 5 may also be helpful.

NEW PROBLEM 2 (60-80 minutes)

Tasty Snacks Limited

Tasty Snacks Limited ("TSL" or the company) is a private company incorporated under the Canada Business Corporations Act. It is entirely owned by Mr. Phil Burns. TSL commences operations on January 1, 19x2 and is financed 50% by a loan from the bank (secured by the accounts receivable and inventory of TSL) and 50% by capital invested by Mr. Burns. Mr. Burns hopes to sell some of the company's shares to the public in a few years. TSL is in the food processing business. Its operations consist of buying fruit commodities such as prunes and apricots in world markets, drying them, and packaging them into units which can be marketed at retail, primarily through the major supermarket chains. The commodities involved lose freshness and deteriorate in other ways with the passage of time, even if dried and packaged in the form of dried fruit. Prices in its buying market are subject to the contingencies of crop conditions in various parts of the world and prices in the retail market are tied fairly closely to the annual world price situation. That is, when world buying market prices for fruit fall, the price of packaged dried fruit tends to fall in supermarkets. As a result, the selling price which TSL receives for its finished product, packaged dried fruit, also falls.

To protect itself from world commodity price fluctuations, TSL arranges some long term purchase contracts with suppliers of fruit. TSL agrees to buy a certain quantity of fruit over the next three years at a fixed purchase price. Prices for fruit are expected to be high for the first half of 19x2, due to a world shortage, but may fall later in 19x2 as crop conditions improve.

The controller of TSL recommends that revenue be recognized upon shipment of packaged dried fruit to the supermarkets. The supermarkets are free to return any packages of dried fruit not considered fresh. TSL officials have no idea how many such returns will occur, since they are lacking any history. The controller recommends that such returns be recognized as a reduction in sales revenue when the return occurs.

During the first few months of 19x2, the company incurs considerable costs ("promotion costs") in advertising and wining and dining supermarket buyers. As a result, production and sales do not commence until April 1, 19x2. The controller recommends that recognition of such advertising and promotion costs be deferred (that is, that the costs should be capitalized as assets) and amortized over the life of the business. He regards the costs as "one time" outlays associated with the starting up of a new business. The controller cites the "matching concept" used by accountants as a defence for this accounting policy.

On January 1, 19x2, the company acquires a building and specialized processing equipment, and hires necessary supervisory staff. The controller recommends that all salaries and bank interest paid between January 1 and April 1, 19x2 be capitalized as "start-up costs" and expensed over five years. In addition, he recommends that depreciation on the building and equipment should commence on April 1, 19x2. The controller again cites the "matching concept" as a defence, explaining that, since there are no sales between January 1 and April 1, 19x2, no expenses should be recognized in this same period.

Required:

Assume the role of accounting advisor to Mr. Burns. Prepare a report to him outlining your responses to the controller's proposed accounting policies. Give accompanying reasoning to support your advice.

A Solution

This case is primarily concerned with conflicts among concepts of stewardship accounting (the objectivity concept versus matching, etc.) in a
start-up situation. It also examines revenue and loss recognition issues
where a perishable product and a fixed purchase contract are involved.
The case is aimed at concepts developed up to and including Chapter 5
of the text. As a result, there will be some issues (such as sales
returns, inventory valuation, and fixed asset depreciation) which are discussed in later chapters, and so will be touched on only briefly in this
solution. At a later stage in the course, students may want to return to
this case and think through issues not fully developed in the following
solution. The solution adheres to the case format outlined in this book
for C3-1 of Chapter 3.

1. <u>Objectives</u> of accounting information are to facilitate:

    a. Loan decision by creditor.

    b. Income tax return preparation.

    The above are the two important objectives of accounting information
    for TSL. The creditor's needs are paramount since the bank provides
    50% of the company's financing requirements. Accounting policies
    should be tailored to suit, first, their needs and then other objec-
    tives. The next most important objective is income tax. Cash is
    presumably scarce (a new company with a large bank loan) and account-
    ing policies which help delay the payment of income tax as well as
    meet other objectives would be helpful. Stewardship and performance
    evaluation are less important objectives because Mr. Burns is an owner-
    manager who knows what is happening. Finally, students may want to
    consider a third objective:

    c. Prediction, a few years hence, by potential investors.

    Mr. Burns wants to sell shares to the public in a few years. At that
    time, a prospectus (a document outlining the offering in a form pre-
    scribed by the provincial securities commissions involved) will be
    required, an underwriter (a financial intermediary who will sell the
    shares for TSL) will have to be sought, an auditor may be required
    at that time, and so on. Therefore, accounting policies selected
    must be defensible in the next few years. Potential investors will
    use earnings trends established in the first few years to estimate
    the longer term outlook for the company. This objective is less
    immediate than the above two, and hence somewhat less important at
    this time.

2. <u>Accounting problems</u> which the accounting advisor may wish to discuss
    are, in order of importance:

    a. Revenue recognition regarding sales to supermarkets.

b. Cost recognition regarding sales returns, which ought to be consistent with the basis of revenue recognition chosen. Students should note that sales returns are discussed in Chapter 7 of the text. An in-depth knowledge of sales returns is not needed at this time.

c. Loss recognition if buying prices for fruit fall below TSL's contract purchase price.

d. Cost recognition regarding advertising and promotion costs.

e. Cost recognition regarding salary, interest, and depreciation costs in the period January 1 to April 1, 19x2.

f. Inventory obsolesence problems (spoiled fruit).

3. Analysis of accounting problems

Problem a. Some alternatives for revenue recognition are:
i. recognition upon shipment (the controller's suggestion);
ii. recognition upon payment of cash by supermarkets;
iii. recognition after a reasonable period elapses and no returns of unsatisfactory products occur.

What do the facts suggest? The company is new. It has a history of sales returns to fall back on for information. Supermarkets are probably reliable customers who pay their bills, provided they are satisfied with the product. Recall our four stewardship tests of revenue recognition in Chapter 5 of the text. Alternative i. would be acceptable when returns can be estimated and accrued for in the same period as the sale, with some "tolerable" accuracy.[1] Since there is no history, an estimate of future sales returns is likely out of the question. TSL may want to consider ii., since payment of cash may serve as a rough proxy indicator that the supermarket is satisfied with the quality of a particular shipment. However, this may be too much of a delay and ultra conservative for some users. Of, if some arrangement can be made such that inspection and return must occur within some number of days after shipment, then perhaps alternative iii. becomes feasible. Obviously, facts are fuzzy and there is room for assumptions by students.

Since facts are fuzzy, let us look to objectives.

The bank loan is secured by accounts receivable and inventory. Students, at this point, should think through the entry required for a return, assuming no previous allowance for returns is set up in

---

[1]Students may wish to refer to Chapter 7 for the accrual entry related to sales returns:

Sales returns (sales revenue –) $XXX
  Accounts receivable, allowance for returns
                              (asset –) $XXX

the accounts (figures are illustrative):

Sales returns (revenue −)* $1,000
  Accounts receivable (asset −) $1,000
To record unsatisfactory merchandise returned
by supermarket.
*Shown as a reduction of sales on the income
statement.

If there was some value to the returned product, the entry to record
the returned inventory would be:

Inventory (asset +) $ 500
  Cost of goods sold (expense −) $ 500

However, for TSL, the returned dried fruit is probably scrapped, and
so this entry is unnecessary. The impact on net income and assets is
therefore the entire $1,000, in this case. (These entries are
described in greater detail in Chapter 7. Do not worry if you do not
understand them fully at this stage. They are not critical to our
answer.)

How would the banker react to such a journal entry, or to a number of
them? The banker may be unhappy, since he relies on the accounts
receivable figure (at least in part) for the loan decision and the
accounts receivable figure may be "overstated" by the amount of
subsequent returns. The banker would probably prefer some delay in
revenue recognition, say alternative iii., since we have assumed a
reasonable estimate of sales returns is not possible.

Looking to our second objective, delay of income tax, a delay in
revenue recognition, alternative iii., would help to postpone income
tax payments. Finally, looking to our third objective, a more conservative recognition such as iii. would help avoid biases in earnings trends caused by early sales recognition and later reduction
in sales. In summary, facts and objectives suggest delay in revenue
recognition until after inspection of the goods, alternative iii.

At this point, students should notice how we use logic and judgment
to select from among alternatives, always looking to facts, objectives and constraints. The latter include legal restrictions, and
generally accepted accounting principles, and so on.

Problem b. This has been discussed above.

Problem c. To see why a loss might occur, students should consider
what happens if the contract purchase price of fruit is $10 a pound,
the current market purchase price of fruit falls to $6 a pound, and
the selling price of dried fruit to supermarkets falls (in response)
to $9 a pound. TSL incurs a loss of $1 a unit, even before any of
TSL's other costs are considered. This could tend to cause wide
swings in TSL's reported earnings. That is, when prices are extremely

low, large losses occur and when prices are extremely high, large gains appear, all due to a fixed supply contract.

The issue for the accounting advisor is when to recognize a loss in the accounting records. This is a somewhat advanced topic for Chapter 5. Students are expected at this stage to recognize the problem, and not much more. As a general rule, accountants do not "accrue" for future operating losses before the period in which they occur. (This is in accordance with the realization concept of stewardship accounting.) To warn bankers who want to predict such events, full disclosure of the contract and its terms (price, quantity, time interval involved) should occur in a note to TSL's first set of financial statements.

Problem d. Some alternatives for advertising and promotion costs are:
i. expense as incurred per the objectivity concept.
ii. expense over the periods which are likely to benefit by the outlays, per the matching concept.

What do the facts suggest? The advertising and promotion expenditures may well be unusually heavy in the first few months. Later sales may be higher as a result (thus suggesting that we match). Is this justification for capitalization as an asset and amortization (especially if the company is new and there is no assurance that it will enjoy the future benefits)? Most accountants would not regard the expenditures as an asset (alternative ii.), because their benefits to future periods cannot be determined with sufficient objectivity. That is, which periods and how many are benefited is anybody's guess. We cannot match these costs with later revenues in a sufficiently meaningful or objective way. Here is an example where the matching concept, if carried to extreme, results in a conflict with the objectivity concept. Therefore, the facts alone suggest alternative i. should be adopted.

What about objectives? The banker probably does not want less objectively measured assets on the balance sheet. Expensing also helps to delay payment of income taxes. Auditors would likely not agree with capitalization because benefits are too uncertain. Consequently, both facts and objectives rule out deferral and amortization of advertising and promotion costs.

Problem e. This was covered to some extent in problem d. Salary and interest costs are poor candidates for capitalization and amortization, even more so than advertising and promotion. Salary and interest are, for TSL, period costs. (See the Appendices to Chapter 4.) They occur whether sales occur or not. Hence, they should be expensed here in the period in which they occur. That is, they cannot be matched with specific sales in any meaningful way. The matching concept does not apply, and has no role to play here.

Depreciation is more complicated, and at this stage in the course we will avoid going into depth. Suffice it to say that depreciation on the building is generally regarded as a period cost (wear and tear probably occurs whether TSL operates or not), and hence should be recorded over the first three months. The need to record depreciation on equipment is debatable. Does the equipment lose its economic value if it is not used in the first three months, purely as a result of elapsed time? If so, record depreciation on equipment for the first three months. If not, a case can be made for no recognition of depreciation expense. The banker probably does not care, as depreciation is a non-cash item; moreover, the income tax department has its own rules for depreciation. Hence, considering our objectives, it does not much matter, at this point, whether or not equipment is depreciated for the first three months.

Problem f. At this stage in the course, all we expect is that students be alert to the inventory problem. If spoilage occurs over time (what are the facts?), should write-downs occur to reflect the decline in eventual selling price below cost? Such a write-down would warn the banker who bases loan decisions in part on recorded inventory balances. A write-down may help to delay income tax payments and conserve cash. Any write-down would increase expenses (expense +), decrease inventory (assets −), and hence would help to delay income tax, which is based on net income. This is an illustration of the realization concept referred to in Chapter 5. That is, recognize the loss when the decline in value has occurred.

4. Recommendations (to problems identified as a., b., etc.)

a.,b. Recognize revenue after goods are inspected for quality by the supermarket, so that unsatisfactory shipments are not prematurely recognized as sales. Here, we attempt to facilitate the objectives of reliable information for creditors and postponement of income tax cash payments.

c. Recognize any operating losses arising out of unfavourable purchase contracts as they occur (realization concept), but disclose details of contracts in a note (full disclosure concept) to facilitate judgments by creditors.

d. Recognize advertising and promotion costs as they are incurred, since no objective (objectivity concept) means exist to match expenses with later revenues (matching concept) and the creditor and income tax objectives are better served by expensing.

e. Recognize salary and interest costs as incurred, since no defensible argument exists for their capitalization, the matching concept does not apply, etc. For similar reasons, recognize building depreciation and possibly equipment depreciation (check the facts first) for the first three months of operations.

f. Recognize inventory obsolescence by a write-down as it is apparent (realization concept). This helps to warn creditors and to delay income taxes.

6 *Valuation of Assets; Cash and Marketable Securities*

IMPORTANT REMINDER

Chapter 6 combines two somewhat different topics: (1) asset valuation in general, and (2) measurement and disclosure issues involving cash and marketable securities. Yet these two topics are related in the sense that income measurement, note disclosure, and valuation have to be tailored to objectives of accounting, facts, and constraints; otherwise, accounting may not serve its desired purpose as a system of communicating information, and unsuitable judgments could result.

Before commencing an explanation of the new concepts in Chapter 6, let us review two recurring themes and build upon Chapter 5. Accounting financial statements are the result of an interaction between the preparer and the user. The interests of these two parties may not coincide, because of conflicting objectives and many other factors, such as the potential legal liability of preparers. Consequently, users have to be careful in interpreting financial data and should not automatically assume that the perhaps general purpose financial statements were assembled solely for their needs.

An understanding of this potential user-preparer conflict is not helped by attitudes and education programs which pretend that a conflict might not exist, or that it does not affect the subject. Some persons who are commencing their learning of accounting tend to seek a non-existent certainty. They want to be able to count "facts which they have learned" or matters which are of lifetime validity. They may inadvertently regard these as "basics", or "the only basics."

In a sense, the balance sheet equation (assets = liabilities + owners' equity) and income statement equation (revenue – expenses = net income) are "basics." However, the *essence* of accounting is knowing the definitions of terms (what is a "liability"?) and their applications. Application requires *judgment*, a skill which requires considerable learning effort on our part. If we try to by-pass judgment, we miss an understanding of the subject.

Acquiring judgment can be a frustrating experience. Often we do not receive immediate feedback, even in a classroom setting, as to whether our judgment decision was sound (or perhaps "correct"). We do not know whether or not we have "learned something lasting." Judgment exercises are unlike directed questions where one receives an ego boost for a "correct" response. Judgment learning requires us to look for general relationships, to learn exceptions, and to build a general model of the subject in our mind. We must always be on guard for revisions to our general model.

Why do we repeat the foregoing theme? There are two main reasons: (1) we have to learn to be patient with ourselves, and to not be pre-occupied with counting "truths" which we "know" that we have learned; and (2) we have to give support to our instructors, who would like to minimize frustration, but can easily *defeat* their learning objectives by frequently switching from judgment exercises to directed questions. Some students can adjust to the less directed setting faster than others. This means that instructors might have to use different approaches in class, depending upon student response. Instructors need accurate feedback from students if they are to accomplish the learning objectives relevant to students' needs. Needless complaints can give instructors a false reading.

Students tend to receive the education which they demand. Instructors are widely outnumbered in a classroom; they must rely on the goodwill of the class until leaders emerge and provide direction for the learning experience. When the class is supportive of a less directed style and approaches other than one-way lecturing, and is willing to tolerate the frustrations of developing judgment, then an approach to this and other subjects, which is valuable for a lifetime, can be learned. In contrast, a demand for "correct" answers, directed questions, high grades, etc., will force the instructor to tailor the course to student desires. As a consequence, students may acquire some knowledge but little ability to assess and apply it.

Large classes, student course evaluations, multiple-section courses, accompanying student desires for uniform treatment across all sections, and similar factors, intimidate instructors. Canada is desperately short of qualified accounting instructors. Excessive demands for bookkeeping and directed questions tend to result in accounting courses which are unrepresentative of reality. Such courses risk providing "rules" that can change tomorrow almost at the whim of a rule-making body.

The choice is yours. Each class has vocal people who want certainty. If you want something else, you will have to speak out in the classroom. Instructors may be able to accomodate different groups by varying their approaches and tailoring them to differing student abilities. They need your help to do so.

PREDICTION OBJECTIVE

The accuracy of predictions can be questioned; but it is pointless for us to pretend that people do not make predictions or that predictions are

not necessary. Major investments in long term assets generally are made
only after some peering into the future occurs. Investors want to know
what yield or return on investment might be expected. If the yield is
appropriate in view of the risk, they would invest their money.

Financial statements of recent periods, by themselves, are not likely
to be accurate indications of future results in a changing environment.
Nevertheless some people use portions of financial statements as an aid
in prediction (current revenue figures sometimes are indications of
future revenues). Many other pieces of information are used to supplement financial data. This is explained later in this chapter under the
heading "Accrual Accounting and Prediction."

Conceptually speaking, those interested in prediction are attempting to
determine the current worth of an entity by discounting the future cash
receipts less cash disbursements over the remaining life of the organization or asset. In order to do this they have to determine: (1) the
amount of cash receipts less disbursements; (2) the *timing* of the cash
flows (because different discount factors are needed for different dates
in the future); and (3) an appropriate discount rate.

Let us illustrate the prediction objective, the value to the user approach
(page 255 of the textbook), and compound interest, in a brief illustration.
Suppose:

1. The following *cash* receipts (for sales) and *cash* disbursements (for
    expenses) are expected over the next three years:

	Cash Receipts	Cash Disbursements
Year 1	$ 70,000	$40,000
Year 2	90,000	45,000
Year 3	100,000	52,000

    For simplicity we will assume that the cash flows occur on the last
    day of each of the three years. Also we will assume that after
    Year 3 no more cash flows occur.

2. In view of the risk (or chance of loss of some or all of your invest-
    ment) an interest rate of 10% per annum seems appropriate.

How much would we pay *today* to acquire this investment? We know the
amount and the timing of the cash flows. Hence, all we have to do is
discount them at the 10% rate. In real, complex companies where we are
not certain of the amount and timing of cash flows, rough approximations
of the discounting approach are used. But, the general concept of worth
still applies. *If* you intend to hold on to an investment, its worth to
you is measured in "value to the user" discounted present value terms.

The present value of the investment at 10% per annum discounting is (see

Appendix to the textbook, Table 2, page 757):

		Factor	Present Value
Year 1:	$ 70,000 - $40,000 = $30,000 x	0.9091 =	$ 27,273
Year 2:	$ 90,000 - $45,000 = $45,000 x	0.8264 =	$ 37,188
Year 3:	$100,000 - $52,000 = $48,000 x	0.7513 =	$ 36,062
	Beginning of Year 1 value to user		$100,523

We can prove that we have received 10% per year on our investment by commencing with the present value ($100,523) and show that annual interest and annual repayments of net cash inflow reduce to zero at the end of the three years.

Present value of investment	$100,523
Interest at 10% for Year 1 on $100,523	10,052
	$110,575
Deduct net cash of $30,000 received at the end of Year 1 (and which represents a repayment of the investment)	30,000
Beginning of Year 2 value	80,575
Interest at 10% for Year 2 on $80,575	8,058
	88,633
Deduct net cash of $45,000 received at the end of Year 2	45,000
Beginning of Year 3 value	43,633
Interest at 10% for Year 3 on $43,633	4,363
	47,996
Deduct net cash of $48,000 received at the end of Year 3	48,000
Difference due to rounding, $4, is not important	$ 0

Although the total cash received, net of disbursements, at the end of the three years is $123,000 ($30,000 plus $45,000 plus $48,000), its present worth is only $100,523 at the 10% interest rate. This present worth would change if our rate of interest was altered, or if our cash flows were measured incorrectly, or if our timing of receipt was not judged accurately. For example, suppose that the cash receipts were reversed: $48,000 at the end of Year 1; $45,000 at the end of Year 2; and $30,000 at the end of Year 3:

Year 1:	$48,000 x 0.9091	=	$ 43,637
Year 2:	$45,000 x 0.8264	=	$ 37,188
Year 3:	$30,000 x 0.7513	=	$ 22,539
	Present Value		$103,364

If we paid $100,523 for the investment and it turned out to generate $103,364 in present value terms, this would mean that we received *more* than 10% interest on our investment. Of course, it is possible that we could receive less cash than $100,523 in present value terms, and consequently, less than 10% on our investment. When the variation (called risk) in what we could receive is great we might ask for more than a 10% interest rate to compensate for possible losses of our initial investment. A higher rate of interest lowers the present value. To illustrate, suppose that a 15% interest rate is chosen, and the net cash flows are as originally stated. The present value would be (See page 757 of the textbook):

$$
\begin{array}{lll}
\text{Year 1:} & \$30,000 \times 0.8696 & = \$26,088 \\
\text{Year 2:} & \$45,000 \times 0.7561 & = \$34,025 \\
\text{Year 3:} & \$48,000 \times 0.6575 & = \underline{\$31,560} \\
& & \underline{\$91,673}
\end{array}
$$

In brief, the interest rate, present value (or investment), and annual cash flows are interrelated and a change in one of them affects the others.

ACCRUAL ACCOUNTING AND PREDICTION

This section may be difficult to understand. If you have trouble with it do not be concerned. Return to it at a later date. Some of the concepts are advanced in scope.

In the previous chapters considerable attention was given to the accrual basis of accounting. How can we reconcile the accrual theme with a prediction objective or purpose of financial accounting? Before we proceed, it is important to remember that the accrual basis was *not* designed for those who want to predict future cash flows and then establish an enterprise's current worth. Such users are merely trying their best with whatever information exists.

In a sense there are two types of accruals or transactions which are particularly noteworthy for the prediction objective:

1. Short-term accruals for accounts receivable, accounts payable, prepaid expense, and so forth. (Cash flows may just be a few days or weeks prior to or after the accrual entry.)

2. Longer term accruals or transactions pertaining to long term investing or financing. (A cash receipt for issuance of long-term debt or shares requires special treatment because the debt plus equity (shares) combination helps determine the discount or interest rate. A cash disbursement for buildings and equipment often can be viewed (as we will see in later courses) as the amount of the *investment* (or present value). Subsequent depreciation of this investment in accordance with accrual accounting is a non-cash item and is ignored when discounting under the prediction objective.

In a complex, real life situation, those who wish to employ discounting in pursuing a prediction objective must estimate income statement effects for subsequent years. As noted in the previous paragraph, accrual income statement figures differ in timing from cash flows. However, in those situations where the accrual is *short term* (such as the collection of cash on accounts receivable, or payment for inventory in advance of its being sold), accrual figures are accepted as equivalent to cash flows. The reason for treating cash and accruals as equals is that the computation tends to be a rough estimate. The discount rate, for instance, is approximate only, not 100% accurate. Also, because discount factors decrease for each future year, errors have less effect on present value.

When the accrual is for a longer term or the accrual figures are well removed in time from cash flows, accruals must be amended for the discounting process. Depreciation expense, for example, would not be used in the computation of annual cash flows.

To illustrate, let us assume the following situation:

1. A company commences business on January 1, 19x1 with $500,000 of a 10 year debt on which it is required to pay 10% interest per annum, and $500,000 of common share equity which is expected to yield 20% per annum.

2. The $1,000,000 from 1. is invested in a project which is expected to generate the following income figures (ignoring income tax) for the next 10 years:

Revenue		$879,251
Cost of goods sold		600,000
Gross profit		279,251
Expenses:		
Selling and Administration	$ 80,000	
Depreciation	100,000	
Interest expense	50,000	230,000
Income		$ 49,251

At the end of 10 years the project is assumed to be worthless.

The point of the illustration is to ascertain, on a discounted basis, whether the common shareholders will receive the 20% return on their equity. In brief, will the above figures prove to be a complete equation which balances?

In order to do the computation we must have an interest rate. Later courses will explain the reasoning underlying what follows, but the appropriate rate in this situation is what results from the combination of debt plus common equity:

Debt: $ 500,000 at 10% annual cost (interest expense) = $ 50,000

Equity: $ 500,000 at 20% annual cost   = $100,000
         $1,000,000 $150,000

$$\text{Average} = \frac{\$\ 150,000}{\$1,000,000} = 15\%$$

The arithmetic is straight-forward, but the implications are tricky. Note that in order to compute the discount rate we had to use the annual *interest expense* figure. This interest expense is a cash outflow which appears on the income statement. But, having used it once in arriving at the interest rate, we cannot use it again in computing annual cash flows. To do so would be to *double count*.

How, then, do we compute annual cash flows (cash receipts less cash disbursements)? As explained earlier, if we ignore the accrual effects of short term cash flows, the accrual approximations of *annual* cash flows (receipts less disbursements) would be:

Revenue – (Cost of goods sold + selling and administration)

$879,251 – ($600,000 + $80,000) = $199,251.

We can discount the $199,251 per year for 10 years by using the figure for 15%, 10 years on page 761 of the textbook. This assumes that the cash flows occur at the *end* of each year.

$199,251 x 5.0188 = $1,000,000

All that this exercise proves is that $199,251 received at the *end* of each of the next 10 years has a present value of $1,000,000 when an interest rate of 15% is used. *But*, that 15% carries a special meaning; it conveys that the bondholders are receiving 10% on their investment, and that the common shareholder is receiving 20%.

Specifically, this means that the bondholder receives $50,000 in interest at the end of each of the 10 years plus $500,000 at the end of the 10th year. The present value of this is (at 10%):

$ 50,000 (10% x $500,000) x 6.1446 (page 761) = $307,230

$500,000 x 0.3855 (page 757)   =   192,750
                                                    499,980
          Rounding difference   20
                                                   $500,000

- 92 -

For the common shareholder the figures are (at 20%)

$$\$100,000 \ (\$500,000 \times 20\% \times .419^* \quad = \quad \$419,000$$
$$500,000 \times .162^* \qquad\qquad\qquad = \qquad \underline{81,000}$$
$$\underline{\underline{\$500,000}}$$

*Not available in your textbook.

The $500,000 for bonds and $500,000 for shares equals the $1,000,000 investment.

In summary, what is important to those who are interested in prediction?

1. The annually-recurring cash flows. These can be approximated by look-ing at the income statement figures, and ignoring non-cash items such as depreciation and payments for interest.

2. The initial investment (such as the $1,000,000 above).

3. The interest or discount rate (which is approximated indirectly by computing the average cost of debt plus equity, as used in the foregoing, or directly by knowing the yield on the investment, which was 15% in the foregoing illustration).

Mainly those interested in prediction are trying to ascertain point 1.

TEXTBOOK *P6-9: A SOLUTION (20-30 minutes)

This question is a little trickier than it may first appear to be. It is not clear at first what is meant by "June deposits" and "June cheques" under the "Per Bank" column. Are the items outstanding at May 31, 19x1 included with the bank's June figures because they were received or cashed by the bank in June? If we make the assumption that the "Per Bank" figures for June do not include the outstanding items at May 31, 19x1, the bank reconciliation at June 30, 19x1 will not balance. Therefore, after what may turn out to be a trial and error process, we can make the assumption that the June "Per Bank" figures include the outstanding items at May 31, 19x1. This is the most logical assumption to make because, in practice, the June bank statement would show most if not all of the outstanding items at May 31. Some cheques outstanding at May 31, 19x1 might also be outstanding at June 30, 19x1. With this latter assumption the bank reconciliation will balance.

a. In view of this latter assumption the outstanding items at May 31, 19x1 would have to be subtracted from the June figures "Per Bank."

	Deposits	Cheques
Per Bank – for June	$15,500	$21,420
Less items outstanding at May 31, 19x1, which pertain to May and earlier	$ 2,000	4,560
June receipts deposited in June	$13,500	
June cheques cashed in June		$16,860

We can compute the outstanding deposits and cheques by comparing the above with the amounts shown "per company books."

	Deposits	Cheques
Per company books – for June	$16,800	$19,730
Less June receipts deposited in bank in June	13,500	
Less June cheques cashed by bank in June		16,860
Outstanding at June 30, 19x1	$ 3,300	$ 2,870

b.
	Deposits	Cheques
Balance per bank statement, June 30, 19x1		19,600
Add:		
Deposits in transit	3,300	
Bank charges	12	3,312
		$22,912
Subtract:		
Outstanding cheques	2,870	
Note collected by bank	2,000	4,870
Balance per general ledger, June 30, 19x1		$18,042

c.
Bank charges (expense +)	$ 12	
Cash	2,000	
Cash		$ 12
Note receivable		2,000

d. Reconciliations check the completeness of the bank deposits, the recording of all cheques, identify bank and company errors, and generally provide a cross-check on the bank account. If reconciliations occur each month, errors can be caught quickly, as can some types of fraud.

7 Receivables and Payables

Much of Chapter 7 is concerned with the valuation of receivables. The basis of valuation which accountants attempt to attain for receivables is net realizable value or cash value. If the receivable is due one year hence or more, it ought to be discounted to a net realizable value in present value dollars.

Many pages in Chapter 7 should be read in conjunction with the main thoughts expressed in Chapter 5, especially the "key accounting concepts." Materiality, matching, revenue recognition, conservatism, etc., have to be considered from both balance sheet and income statement points of view. Revenue recognition or realization methods were chosen after considering applicable objectives, facts, and constraints, primarily from an income statement viewpoint. Chapter 7 spends time on a balance sheet viewpoint, and the treatments chosen for various issues might temper the income statement effects.

For example, such matters as the handling of potentially uncollectible accounts, sales returns, and cash discounts, affect the valuation of receivables as well as net income. It is possible, for instance, to significantly alter a basis of revenue recognition by choosing a quite different policy of providing for uncollectible accounts. A large provision (and charge to income) for uncollectible accounts combined with a policy of recognizing revenue on delivery of goods might have virtually the same income statement effect as a policy of recognizing revenue only on collection of cash. That is why we have to view the concepts in Chapter 5 and 7 together -- they could offset each other.

Question 7-2 in the textbook examines the foregoing theme. Subsequent problems provide practice with the accounting cycle.

TEXTBOOK *7-2: A SOLUTION (15-25 minutes)

Certain key accounting concepts can be used to justify making estimates, wherever possible, of future uncollectibles:

Matching concept - an estimate of bad debts should be reflected as an

expense in the same period as related revenue is
recognized.

Realization concept – losses should be recognized when they are realized;
that is, when the decline in value has occurred and
is capable of reasonable estimation. Bad debt
losses should be recognized when the uncollectible
first becomes apparent.

Conservatism – provide for all known or estimable losses. (This concept
is modified in a later chapter when we discuss "contingencies".)

It is not necessary to know which particular account is likely to be
uncollectible. Estimates can be applied to total receivables. Hence,
the argument posed in the quotation is not a strong one.

The question hints at a potential conflict between the objectivity concept (estimates of revenue and bad debts should be capable of objective
and reasonably accurate estimation) and other concepts mentioned above.
The latter suggest timely recognition of revenue and estimable bad debt
losses so as to make financial statement figures relevent for readers.
This is an example of the objectivity versus relevance conflict mentioned
in the text. If estimates are too subjective, subsequent errors in
estimates may alarm readers (say, perhaps, a banker who relied on accounts
receivable figures to make a loan decision). If this is the case, perhaps
no estimate of bad debts should be made and revenue should be recognized
as cash is received. However, this latter method (known as the cash basis
of revenue recognition) may not provide sufficient timely, relevant information on sales and receivables for those (say, investors) who want to
predict future earnings. Notice how objectives conflict here. The banker
may want objective, accurate information, and hence may favour delay in
recognition so as to minimize errors in estimate. The investor wants
timely, relevant information about expected cash flows from sales, and
hence may favour early recognition of sales with some estimate of bad debts.
Perhaps the investor can tolerate a reasonably wide margin of error in an
estimate of bad debts (say, +10%), whereas the banker may not be able to
tolerate such a margin.

How does the accountant resolve such a conflict in objectives? He attempts
to rank objectives in order of importance, and, where possible, use full
note disclosure to help cater to all user groups. For example, where
recognition of revenue is delayed to a cash basis, the accountant may
elect to disclose in a note what sales are for the year on some other
basis of revenue recognition. Investors may be able to predict on the
basis of information in notes, especially if stock markets are "efficient."
This might occur when investors are quick to grasp information regardless
of where it is disclosed, in the body of the financial statements or in
a footnote.

Question 7-2 hinted at the effect of different revenue recognition points
on bad debts. The question below deals directly with this theme.

Situation 1:

A Ltd. sells equipment, on account, to about 200 retail dealers.
Historical trends indicate that 3% of all sales are eventually uncollectible. A reveiw of 19x1 accounts receivable indicates that this is a
reasonable assumption for 19x1 sales. A Ltd. recognizes revenue upon
shipment to dealers. Accordingly, in 19x1 it recognizes a bad debt
expense of $60,000 on $2,000,000 of sales (with an original cost of goods
sold of $1,300,000) for the year. In 19x2, $55,000 of the 19x1 sales
prove to be uncollectible, relating to several dealers, and the amounts
are written off. The remainder of the cash relating to 19x1 sales is
collected early in 19x2.

Situation 2:

B Ltd. sells clothes to customers who "come in off the street." A select
group of credit-worthy customers are allowed to purchase on account, and
pay in 30 days. In the past, uncollectibles have been known to occur,
even among this select group of customers. The rate of uncollectibles
tends to be unpredictable., depending in part on swings in the economy.
To be "conservative" (and help delay income tax payments), the owner-
manager of B Ltd. recognizes revenue when cash is received. In January,
19x1, sales of $10,000 (with an original cost of goods sold of $5,000)
are made on account. In February, 19x1, all but $500 of the receivables,
relating to one customer, is collected. In January, 19x2, B Ltd. gives
up trying to collect the $500, and is unable to reclaim the clothes.
B Ltd. has a bank loan outstanding, secured by the personal guarantee
of the owner.

Situation 3:

Assume the same facts as in Situation 1. In 19x2, $60,000 of accounts
receivable from 19x1 sales are written off, all relating to one dealer.
A Ltd. is informed that the dealer has gone bankrupt and collection is
unlikely. In 19x3, to A Ltd.'s surprise, it receives a cheque of
$3,000 from the trustee in bankruptcy, who explains that all creditors
are receiving 5¢ for every one dollar owed. A Ltd. is a public company, whose shares are widely and actively traded. It also has a substantial loan from the bank, secured by inventories and receivables.

Required:

a. Prepare journal entries to record the above transactions.

b. Explain why you feel the method of accounting in each situation
   makes sense given facts and objectives of accounting information
   (and any constraints you can think of).

A Solution

a. Situation 1:

19x1

1.

Accounts receivable (asset +)	$2,000,000	
Sales revenue (revenue +)		$2,000,000

To record the sale of goods and services.
This is a summary entry of numerous
transactions.

2.

Cost of goods sold (expense +)	$1,300,000	
Inventory (asset –)		$1,300,000

To record cost of goods sold in the same
period that revenue is recognized.

3.

Bad debt expense (expense +)	$ 60,000	
Accounts receivable, allowance for		
uncollectibles (asset contra +)		$ 60,000

To establish an allowance for uncollectibles,
based on 3 percent of 19x1 sales. This is
a contra account shown as a reduction to
accounts receivable.

19x2

4.

Cash (asset +)	$1,945,000	
Accounts receivable (asset –)		$1,945,000

To record cash collections relating to
19x1 sales.

5.

Accounts receivable – allowance for uncollect-		
ibles (asset contra +)	$ 55,000	
Accounts receivable (asset –)		$ 55,000

To write off specific accounts.

Students should note that A Ltd. over-provided for bad debt expense in
19x1. In practice, accountants typically leave this in the allowance
account as a cushion for later errors which might go the other way.
The $5,000 is probably a tolerable error in estimate.

Situation 2:

January, 19x1

No entry is required to reflect shipments to customers. Revenue is recognized when cash is collected. (For internal control purposes, a memo could be made in the accounts to indicate who holds the inventory item.)

February, 19x1

1.

Cash (asset +)	$ 9,500	
Sales (revenue +)		$ 9,500

To record sales, as cash is received, from credit customers who received their merchandise in January.

2.

Cost of goods sold (expense +)	$ 4,750	
Inventory (asset −)		$ 4,750

To record cost of goods sold in the same period as related revenue is recognized.

Students should notice that no cost of goods sold is recognized immediately on the $500 worth of merchandise whose sale has not yet been recorded because cash has not been received. This is in accordance with the matching concept.

Sometime in 19x1 (when the loss becomes apparent)

3.

Cost of goods sold (expense +)	$ 250	
Inventory (asset −)		$ 250

To record a recognized loss on inventory, related to an account which will not be collected. This is in accordance with the conservatism concept.

Students should observe that we did not wait until 19x2 to record the loss on the merchandise which is not recovered from the customer. In accordance with the conservatism concept, we record the loss when it is known with reasonable certainty that a loss has occurred. In addition, timely recognition helps save income taxes in 19x1.

Students should also note that this loss recognition does not violate the matching concept, which states in general that the recognition of costs should accompany recording of sales revenue. Losses, which are not the same as expenses, are recognized when they can be measured. A loss is defined as a cost which does not generate revenue. In contrast, an expense is a cost incurred in generating revenue. Loss recognition is discussed later in the textbook in connection with contingencies.

Situation 3:

19x1

The journal entries are the same as in Situation 1.

4.

Cash (asset +)	$1,940,000	
Accounts receivable (asset −)		$1,940,000

To record cash collection relating to 19x1
sales.

5.

Accounts receivable, allowance for uncollectibles (asset contra −)	$ 60,000	
Accounts receivable (asset −)		$ 60,000

To write off a specific account because the
dealer is bankrupt.

6.

Accounts receivable (asset +)	$ 3,000	
Accounts receivable, allowance for uncollectibles (asset contra +)		$ 3,000

To restore part of the account balance
previously written off.

7.

Cash (asset +)	$ 3,000	
Accounts receivable (asset −)		$ 3,000

To record the collection of cash arising
from the bankruptcy settlement for a dealer.
(5¢ on every dollar)

Students should note that it is first necessary to correct the "error"
made in writing off the account prematurely. The best information now
available to the company indicates that it acted too hastily in writing off the account in 19x2. Once the 19x2 write-off entry has been
reversed, collection can be accounted for in the usual manner. The
important point to note is that the premature write-off does not
affect net income in 19x2. The account was fully provided for in 19x1
by the bad debt expense entry. In 19x2, the write off affects only
accounts receivable and its contra allowance. Expense is not affected.
In 19x3, the reversal of the write-off again only affects the two
asset accounts and not expense. Similarly, the collection of cash
affects only cash and accounts receivable.

So why does a premature write-off matter? Leaving the amount in
accounts receivable as long as possible makes sure the receivable is
not forgotten about, thus facilitating the internal control objective
of accounting.

As in Situation 1, there is a small excess provision of $3,000 in the allowance account relating to 19x1 sales. That is, A Ltd. provided for $60,000 of bad debt expense in 19x1 related to 19x1 sales, and $57,000 of this eventually (two years later) proved to be uncollectible. Accountants typically leave an amount this small in the allowance account as a cushion for later errors which may be in the other direction. Suppose that the required allowance at the end of 19x3 is $30,000, based on a review of receivables at that time. If after the necessary entry there is $33,000 in the allowance, $3,000 of which relates to our 19x1 excess provision, the extra $3,000 may be regarded as a satisfactory allowance for any unanticipated bad debt losses. However, other accountants may feel that $30,000 is sufficient and in effect take the $3,000 into income in 19x3 (by reducing bad debt expense in 19x3), thus correcting excess expense recognition in 19x1. Which method is correct? It is a matter of preference and judgment as to what users would want. Bankers would probably prefer the $3,000 cushion. A higher allowance may help delay income tax payments, since 19x3 bad debt expense is higher. Investors may not want too much conservatism, but $3,000 might not matter. Certainly, materiality matters. Had the excess provision related to 19x1 been $20,000 and not $3,000, accountants would recognize the $20,000 as a reduction of bad debt expense in 19x3.

The bad debt entry needed in 19x3 to reflect a $30,000 required allowance would then be (assuming that $20,000 is the average balance in the allowance account before the entry to reflect the necessary balance at the end of 19x3):

Bad debt expense (expense +) $10,000
  Accounts receivable, allowance for
    uncollectibles (asset contra +) $10,000
To bring the balance in the allowance up to
the required $30,000.

Had there been no over-provision in 19x1, the required entry above would be $30,000. It is in this sense that the $20,000 over provision related to 19x1 is recorded as income in 19x3. Hence, any over or under provisions for bad debts can cause serious errors in year to year net income over several years.

b. For A Ltd., recognizing revenue upon shipment to dealers and accruing for any bad debt expense related to that revenue makes sense given objectives, facts, and constraints. Regarding facts, bad debts can be estimated with sufficient objectivity that it makes sense to recognize revenue upon shipment and make a provision for bad debt losses. This choice also satisfies the constraint of generally accepted accounting principles. Regarding objectives, investors would probably appreciate this early recognition of income. Does the banker suffer? Not likely, since our estimate of bad debt losses is reasonably accurate.

For B Ltd., recognizing revenue upon receipt of cash also makes sense. Regarding facts, bad debts cannot be estimated with sufficient

objectivity at the time of delivery. Regarding objectives, the
banker is probably happier with delay of revenue recognition. He
does not want surprises, especially those which involve losses. The
delay helps postpone payment of income taxes, another objective.
"GAAP" constraints would probably allow this method as long as the
facts are as stated above.

New Problem 2, below, is a review problem which seeks to test the
student's grasp of some of the Chapter 7 material as well as provide
a refresher on T-accounts and journal entries. The problem requires
several assumptions to provide missing information. A review of the
material in Chapter 4 of this book should help provide an appropriate
technique for solving this type of problem.

NEW PROBLEM 2 (30-50 minutes)

Compute the opening balance in accounts receivable from the following
information. State your assumptions:

Accounts receivable - closing balance	$ 45,000
Cash paid by a trustee in bankruptcy relating to an account written off in the previous year	$ 3,000
Goods returned from customers during the year (all goods are scrapped upon their return)	$ 6,000
Cash collected from customers during the year, including cash sales	$150,000
Sales revenue	$152,000
Cash sales	$ 3,000
Allowance for sales returns - opening balance	$ 10,000
Allowance for sales returns - closing balance	$ 20,000
Allowance for uncollectibles - opening balance	$ 12,000
Allowance for uncollectibles - closing balance	$ 11,000
Bad debt expense for the year	$ 5,000

A Solution

The basic approach for this type of problem is to reconstruct the journal
entries which occurred during the year and post them to T-accounts. We
have to ask ourselves what is the most logical transaction to affect
each account and alter its balance. Let us set up T-accounts and reconstruct and post journal entries, making assumptions where necessary:

Accounts receivable

Opening	58,000	3,000	(2)	
(1)	3,000	9,000	(4)	
(8)	149,000	6,000	(5)	
		147,000	(7)	
Closing	45,000			

Cash

(2)	3,000
(7)	150,000

Allowance for sales returns

		10,000	Opening
(5)	6,000	16,000	(6)
		20,000	Closing

Sales revenue

3,000	(7)
149,000	(8)

Allowance for uncollectibles

		12,000	Opening
		3,000	(1)
		5,000	(3)
(4)	9,000		
		11,000	Closing

Sales returns

16,000	(6)

Bad debt expense

(3)	5,000

Accounts receivable (asset +) $ 3,000
  Allowance for uncollectibles (asset contra +) $ 3,000
To restore the account previously written off.

2.

Cash (asset +) $ 3,000
  Accounts receivable (asset -) $ 3,000
To record the collection of cash related to
an account previously written off.

3.

Bad debt expense (expense +) $ 5,000
  Allowance for uncollectibles (asset contra +) $ 5,000
To record the bad debt expense and its offsetting
credit.

4.

Allowance for uncollectibles (asset contra -) $ 9,000
  Accounts receivable (asset -) $ 9,000
To write off specific accounts.

The assumption here is that the amount needed to balance the allowance
account must relate to write-offs. What else could it relate to?

5.

Allowance for sales returns (asset contra -) $ 6,000
  Accounts receivable (asset -) $ 6,000
To give the customer credit for merchandise
returned.

6.

Sales returns (revenue -) $16,000
  Allowance for sales returns (asset contra +) $16,000
To record the estimate of sales returns.

The assumption here is that the amount needed to balance the allowance for
sales returns account must relate to the expense entry for the year. Once
again, what else could it relate to?

7.

Cash (asset +) $150,000
  Sales revenue (cas sales) $ 3,000
  Accounts receivable (asset -)   147,000
To record cash collected from customers for
the year.

We have assumed that the difference between cash collected and cash sales relates to collections of accounts receivable (a reasonable assumption).

8.

Accounts receivable (asset +)	$149,000	
Sales revenue (revenue +)		$149,000

To record sales on account for the year.

We have assumed that the difference between the total sales and cash sales must relate to sales on account. With that, we are done and the opening accounts receivable is calculated as follows:

> Since opening balance + debits – credits = closing balance,
>
> therefore opening balance = closing balance + credit – debits
>
> $$= \$45,000 + \$165,000 - \$152,000$$
>
> $$= \$58,000$$
>
> Check: $58,000 + $152,000 – $165,000 = $45,000.

Students should note that asset contra accounts like our two allowance accounts in this question serve to reduce accounts receivable to a net figure. Balance sheet presentation might be:

Assets

Current assets		
Cash		$ XXX
Accounts receivable	$45,000	
Less: allowance for uncollectibles	(11,000)	
Less: allowance for sales returns	(20,000)	14,000

In practice, the $14,000 net figure is usually shown opposite accounts receivable and the other figures are not shown.

8 *Inventories and Cost of Goods Sold*

Chapter 8 expands on the themes noted in chapter 5, especially the one concerning the importance of objectives or purposes of accounting, facts, and constraints, in the selection of suitable inventory valuation methods. Inventory can be valued or priced on many different bases, some of which are noted below in Exhibit 1.

EXHIBIT 1

Inventory Valuation Bases and Combinations

A. Merchandising or Trading Companies

Cost Choices	How Cost Applied?	Market Choices	Lower of Cost or Market Apply?
* FIFO	* Gross or net of cash discounts?	* Buying market: – reproduction cost – replacement cost	* Yes or no?
* LIFO			* Applied to individual items or only in total?
* Weighted average	* Periodic or perpetual method		
* Specific identification	* Retail method used to approximate cost?	* Selling market: – net realizable value	

B. Manufacturing Companies:

Besides the above, various additional alternatives exist for determining "cost" of manufactured inventory. For example, depreciation on factory machinery (called "fixed factory overhead") may be regarded as a period cost and not added to the cost of inventory. These additional alternatives are covered in subsequent accounting courses.

Given the existence of many different methods and combinations of arriving at (1) balance sheet figures for inventory and (2) a sum for cost of goods sold, our attention has to be directed to where each method or combination can be sensibly applied. What is suitable for a simple stewardship objective is not likely to be useful as an aid in prediction. Chapter 8 in the textbook introduces both the methods of computation and where each might apply. However, most students have difficulty fully grasping where each method or alternative applies. Do not be overly concerned if you have such difficulty at this stage; clarity comes with practice.

The historic cost choices (such as FIFO and LIFO) tend to be used when a stewardship report is needed or a constraint such as "generally accepted accounting principles" applies. For income tax purposes, LIFO may not be used in Canada. If prediction or evaluation of management by outsiders is an objective, then replacement cost and net realizable value are helpful. Additional broad guidance is provided in the textbook.

Textbook question *8-12, attempts to place all of the foregoing discussion or measurement in perspective. Measurement of income is necessary in order to comply with, for example, the income tax objective of accounting. But some other objectives, such as attempts at cash flow prediction, might be satisfactorily accommodated by note disclosure in financial statements. Students should be alert to where measurement is directly on financial statements, and where disclosure is (1) necessary, and (2) helpful.

TEXTBOOK *8-12: A SOLUTION (10-20 minutes)

Chapter 8 of the text discusses "stock market efficiency"; students should refer to that discussion. To briefly summarize that discussion, the basic idea behind "efficient stock markets" is that share prices react quickly and in an "unbiased" fashion to publicly available information. By "unbiased," we mean that investors are often able to separate information from non-information, and that the share price fully reflects that information content. Financial statements make up an important subset of the publicly available information about some companies. If the market for the share is "efficient," the investors as a group will be able to separate information from non-information in financial statements. Data disclosed in a footnote to the financial statements may include important information for investors who want to predict (for example, data on important contracts or unusual events, and so on). It might not matter to an efficient market where in the financial statements such information is disclosed (in a footnote or in the body of the financial statements), as long as the information is there. The share price will adjust accordingly. As mentioned in the text, investors can be fairly capable of recognizing the magnitude of net income differences caused by different inventory costing methods. They may not be tricked into using "non-information," such as inappropriate costing methods, for inventory.

Is the market for most Canadian shares efficient? Our best answer to date, based on research, is that the market for some shares in Canada, mainly for large and widely traded companies, is efficient. Even for these shares, users may vary along a continuum of perceptiveness. Large

scale investors, analysts and creditors are probably at one end
(sophisticated and perceptive), and employees and other unsophisticated
readers are probably at the other end (the so called "naive" users).
This continuum can be represented as in Exhibit 2.[1]

EXHIBIT 2

SCALE OF USER PERCEPTIVENESS REGARDING
UNDERLYING ECONOMIC EVENTS AND CONDITIONS
NOT CLEARLY, CONSISTENTLY, OR UNIFORMLY
REPORTED IN FINANCIAL STATEMENTS

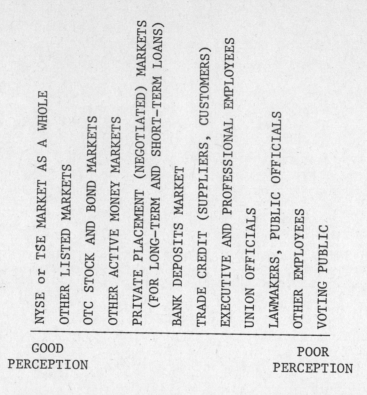

GOOD
PERCEPTION

POOR
PERCEPTION

It is crucial that students see that accounts, facing reporting problems,
must make some assumptions about the perceptiveness of specific anticipated users in a given situation. Judgment therefore must be developed
as early as possible, if one is to be a good preparer or user of accounting statements.

In some situations, readers may be assumed to be highly perceptive (similar
to the concept of "efficient"), and reporting and disclosure can be tailored
accordingly. In other situations, the accountant may have reason to believe

[1]FASB Research Report, *Economic Consequences of Financial Accounting
Standards - Selected Papers,* (Stamford, Connecticut: Financial Accounting
Standards Board, July 1978), Page V of the Introduction.

that readers are naive, in which case there is a need to protect such readers from unwise decisions by careful selection of reporting and disclosure. Such careful selection might differ from the reporting and disclosure selection that is based on an assumption of high user perceptiveness. For example, conservative revenue recognition policies may be best for a small private company whose aging sole owner is relying on the investment in the company to retire on, and who might otherwise be hurt by subsequent and unanticipated bad debts or losses. On the other hand, given a large public company with the same set of transactions and facts, more timely recognition of revenue (or at least disclosure of otherwise unavailable information about revenues) might better satisfy readers who want to predict. Conservatism may not be desired by such readers.

The importance for inventory valuation, as mentioned earlier, is that different stewardship methods (LIFO, FIFO, etc.) may be devoid of information content if underlying cash flows are the same regardless of the method chosen. That is, an efficient market may "see through" the method chosen and security prices will reflect only investor expectations about future cash flows, such as net realizable value. As a corollary, any information that is not otherwise available to the market but that allows the investors to better predict cash flows (such as disclosed replacement cost and net realizable values) may be worthwhile, provided that 1) the cost of such disclosures is justified by resulting benefits to the company and users of statements in a particular situation, and that 2) the information can somehow be disclosed so that the constraints of generally accepted accounting principles are not violated.

When it is believed that naive users or investors may have access to a financial statement, preparers and auditors become concerned about legal liability. In such situations, constraints such as generally accepted accounting principles and corporate legislation apply.

Problem 1., below, will deal with two different inventory valuation methods (LIFO and FIFO), their impact on recorded net assets (net asset, or asset and liability, valuation issues), and their impact on recorded owners' equity (capital maintenance issues).

NEW PROBLEM 1 (50-70 minutes)

XYZ company is formed in 19x1 with $1,000 invested by two partners. Consider the following information on purchases and sales for the year:

XYZ Company
Purchases and Sales of a Particular Item

Date	Purchases Units	Unit cost	Total	Sales Units	Unit price	Total	Balance Units
1/ 1/19x1	200	$5	$1,000				200
2/15/19x1				100	$12	$1,200	100
4/ 1/19x1	100	$7	$ 700				200
7/15/19x1				100	$12	$1,200	100
12/31/19x1	100	$9	$ 900				200
	400		$2,600	200		$2,400	

Unit selling prices are fixed for 19x1 by contract at $12. All sales are cash sales and all purchases are cash purchases.

Required:

a. Prepare journal entries to record the above transactions assuming that the firm uses perpetual inventory procedures and the following inventory valuation methods:

   i.   FIFO
   ii. LIFO

b. Explain how your answer would differ if periodic inventory procedures were used.

c. Discuss how each inventory valuation method affects net asset valuation and recorded owners' equity.

d. For XYZ Company, which of the above two inventory valuation methods (FIFO or LIFO) would be most appropriate, in relation to relevant objectives, facts, and constraints?

A Solution

a. Required journal entries:

Transaction	FIFO	LIFO

1/ 1/19x1 Purchases	Inventory $1,000
	  Cash $1,000
		Inventory $1,000
		  Cash $1,000

2/12/19x1 Sales	Cash $1,200
	  Sales $1,200
	Cost of goods sold $ 500*
	  Inventory $ 500
	*100 units at $5 each
		Cash $1,200
		  Sales $1,200
		Cost of goods sold $ 500*
		  Inventory $ 500
		*100 units at $5 each

4/ 1/19x1 Purchases	Inventory $ 700
	  Cash $ 700
		Inventory $ 700
		  Cash $ 700

7/15/19x1 Sales	Cash $1,200
	  Sales $1,200
	Cost of goods sold $ 500*
	  Inventory $ 500
	*100 units at $5 each
		Cash $1,200
		  Sales $1,200
		Cost of goods sold $ 700*
		  Inventory $ 700
		*100 units at $7 each

12/31/19x1 Purchases	Inventory $ 900
	  Cash $ 900
		Inventory $ 900
		  Cash $ 900

A summary of the above journal entries is as follows:

FIFO		LIFO	
Cost of goods sold:		Cost of goods sold:	
100 units at $5 =	$ 500	100 units at $5 =	$ 500
100 units at $5 =	500	100 units at $7 =	700
	$1,000		$1,200
Ending inventory:		Ending inventory:	
100 units at $9 =	$ 900	100 units at $5 =	$ 500
100 units at $7 =	$ 700	100 units at $9 =	$ 900
	$1,600		$1,400
Total assets	$2,400	Total assets	$2,200
Owners' equity:		Owners' equity:	
Invested capital:		Invested capital:	
Partner A	$ 500	Partner A	$ 500
Partner B	$ 500	Partner B	$ 500
Retained earnings	$1,400*	Retained earnings	$1,200*
	$2,400		$2,200
*Sales	$2,400	*Sales	$2,400
Cost of goods sold	1,000	Cost of goods sold	1,200
	$1,400		$1,200

b. If periodic inventory procedures are used, the cost of goods sold
entry is made at the end of the accounting period (monthly, quarterly,
annually, or whatever) after physical inventories are taken. This is
in contrast to the perpetual method, where a cost of goods sold entry
is made each time a sale is recognized. For FIFO, as mentioned in the
text, inventory valuation is the same under either the perpetual or
periodic method. For LIFO, however, ending inventory and cost of
goods sold would be calculated as follows for XYZ Company:

Periodic Method

LIFO

Ending inventory		Cost of goods sold	
100 units at $5 =	$ 500	100 units at $9 =	$ 900
100 units at $5 =	500	100 units at $7 =	$ 700
	$1,000		$1,600

Notice how LIFO cost of goods sold is $1,600 under the periodic method
and $1,200 under the perpetual method. Why is there a difference?
Under periodic LIFO, units sold are assumed to have come from the
very last lots purchased in the year. Under perpetual LIFO, units

sold are assumed to have come from the very last lots purchased in the year. Under perpetual LIFO, units sold are assumed to have come from the lots purchased most recently before the sale occurs.

Which method, periodic or perpetual, is better? It mainly depends on the facts. If there are few purchases and sales, as for XYZ Company, the perpetual method is practical and makes sense. Internal control is facilitated, since items are kept track of at the time of each sale. Discrepancies between general ledger inventory balances and a physical count of inventory are reduced. A small business may not want to bother with perpetual records because there may be little need to effect internal controls. Also, a small business may be primarily concerned with an income tax objective of accounting and LIFO is not permissible; hence, cost of goods sold under FIFO is not affected by the perpetual vs. periodic controversy.

c. Using the FIFO method, notice that, for the cost of goods sold entry, units sold are assumed to have come from the earliest purchases, in this case the first lot on 1/1/19x1. Ending inventory is assumed to consist of the latest purchases, in this case the two shipments purchased on 4/1/19x1 and 12/31/19x1. Notice that, if the partners withdraw the entire retained earnings for 19x1 in the form of cash (assume that they could borrow from the bank to do so), XYZ Company will be left with invested capital of $1,000. This amount no longer represents the capital needed to acquire 200 units of inventory at the current replacement cost of $9 each.

An "erosion" of capital of $800 has occurred, computed as follows: ($9-$5) $4 per unit increase times 200 units, or $800. We say that invested capital has not been maintained. If the partners were to withdraw their $1,000 invested capital at the end of 19x1, in cash, this $1,000 of capital could not longer purchase 200 units of inventory. This is one of the limitations of the FIFO method. It allows what are called inflationary holding gains (the difference between purchase price at time of purchase and purchase price at time of sale to be included in net income, which is available (cash permitting) for distribution to shareholders. This failure to maintain capital is measured by taking different maintenance concepts. Chapter 16 discusses capital maintenance in greater depth than does Chapter 8.

Using the LIFO method, notice that units sold are assumed to have come from the latest purchases prior to the date of sale. Ending inventory is assumed to consist of the earliest purchases. In this case, there are still 100 units on hand from the first purchase ($5 each). The other 100 units on hand must come from the 12/31/19x1 purchase ($9 each), since we assume under the perpetual method that the items purchased on 4/1/19x1 are sold. Notice that FIFO ending inventory is greater than LIFO ending inventory in a period of rising purchase prices. This follows directly from the LIFO assumption that the earliest goods purchased are the ones in ending inventory.

For the same reason, notice that FIFO costs of goods sold is less
than that for LIFO. This follows directly from the LIFO assumption
that the latest goods purchased are sold first. In that LIFO matches
more recent costs against sales, some accountants feel that LIFO helps
eliminate some inflationary holding gains from appearing in current
income. (LIFO cost of goods sold may differ from replacement cost of
goods sold when the company purchases inventory infrequently.) Only
replacement cost of goods sold eliminates *all* holding gains.

In inflationary times, when LIFO cost of goods sold is higher than
FIFO cost of goods sold, net income available for distribution to
partners is lower under LIFO. Hence, LIFO may help to reduce the
amount of cash paid out as withdrawals. Such cash may be needed in
the business to replace inventory at current replacement costs.
However, not even LIFO succeeds entirely in "protecting" initial
invested capital. To see this, notice that a complete withdrawal by
partners of LIFO net income leaves $1,000 as invested capital, which
we showed above is insufficient to purchase 200 units at $9 each.
In order to remedy this, some accountants advocate that units be
charged to cost of goods sold at their replacement cost as of the
date of sale, and capital maintenance (owner's equity) be measured
differently. (See Chapter 16).

d. First, we must consider the objectives or purposes of inventory
    accounting. XYZ Company is a partnership. It has no creditors.
    Stewardship is probably important, perhaps to arrive at a so-called
    "objective" net income figure which partners divide between themselves.
    Cash flow prediction is probably not important, since no potential
    investors seem to exist and the partners are familiar with the busi-
    ness. The postponing of income tax payments may be an important
    objective.

    Both FIFO and LIFO are stewardship methods of inventory valuation.
    LIFO is not allowed for income tax purposes. Hence, the above
    objectives of accounting do not fully help us resolve the choice
    between methods, unless we assume that income tax postponement is
    the sole objective, and choose FIFO.

    Let us consider other objectives. During a period of increasing
    replacement costs of inventory, LIFO results in a higher cost of
    goods sold figure, and hence a lower net income, than does FIFO.
    Is this what the partners want? If their objective is to preserve
    invested capital (a capital maintenance viewpoint) they may want to
    choose LIFO because a lower retained earnings figure means less
    earnings available for withdrawal, in effect helping them to retain
    needed cash or other assets in the business. On the other hand, if
    their objective is to get cash out of the company as fast as possible
    (perhaps they only see themselves in business for two or three years),
    LIFO makes less sense and FIFO should be considered. That is, LIFO
    lowers net income and may affect the attitude of partners in making
    withdrawals from invested capital as opposed to income.

FIFO results in an ending inventory balance which is a better approximation of recent costs than is provided by LIFO. This may be important where a bank loan exists, perhaps secured by inventory, and the banker is trying to get some, perhaps naive, impression of the "value" of inventory. During a period of rapidly rising prices, LIFO can result in an unrealistically low ending inventory balance. Perhaps this could hurt the company's ability to get the desired size of loan. Will the company's banker be perceptive? Will she see through to the income and asset valuation effects of LIFO versus FIFO? Perhaps yes, perhaps no. Of course, net realizable values (an indicator of future cash *inflows* from inventory) would be even better for the banker's purposes. But write-ups to net realizable value are not presently allowed by generally accepted accounting principles. Perhaps she can get these by way of a special report from the company. And she may also ask in the same special report for current replacement costs of inventory, to help project future cash *outflows* for inventory.

Next is a short problem illustrating the effects of declining costs on LIFO versus FIFO.

NEW PROBLEM 2 (10-10 minutes)

Assume the same facts as given in 8-A, except that unit costs are $9, $7, and $5 for the purchase lots of 1/1/19x1, 4/1/19x1, and 12/31/19x1 respectively.

Required:

Compute cost of goods sold and ending inventory under:

a. FIFO, and
b. LIFO, cost flow assumptions.

Assume that the company uses periodic inventory procedures.

A Solution

Periodic Method, FIFO

Ending inventory:

100 units at $5 = $ 500
100 units at $7 =   700
               $1,200

Cost of goods sold:

200 units at $9 = $1,800

Periodic Method, LIFO

Ending inventory:

200 units at $9 = $1,800

Cost of goods sold:

100 units at $5 = $ 500
100 units at $7 = $ 700
               $1,200

Notice how LIFO cost of goods sold is now *less* than FIFO cost of goods sold, and LIFO ending inventory is now *more* than FIFO ending inventory. Why is this? Costs of replacing inventory are falling. LIFO matches the most recent, lower, costs against revenue and assigns the earliest, higher, costs to ending inventory. FIFO does the opposite.

Can you see any problems with this? Think about it before you read on. LIFO results in an overstatement of ending inventory when costs are falling, because units are carried at amounts in excess of year end replacement cost. In this case, year end (December 31, 19x1) replacement costs are $5 each. A write-down from $1,800 to $1,000 may be in order, if the company follows the method of lower of cost or replacement cost. Accountants normally recommend a write-down to replacement costs because selling prices typically fall in response to fall in replacement costs.

Suppose the 19x2 selling price for inventory of XYZ Company is contracted already at $9 per unit. Rather than wait until 19x2 to record zero profit on the 200 units in inventory (book cost is $9 each), many accountants would warn readers of financial statements by directly writing the 200 units down to $5 at the end of 19x1. If the write-down did not occur in 19x1, readers might expect a normal profit margin from 19x1 inventory in 19x2 and will be unfavourably surprised when no profit occurs. This, of course, creates difficulties for those interested in the prediction objective. Notice how our write-down to $5 allows for something close to a "normal" profit margin in 19x2 (a $9 selling price less a book cost of $5 each).

The next problem is concerned with the different effects on cost of goods sold, and ending inventory of several costing methods, and the relationship of these methods to the lower of cost or market.

NEW PROBLEM 3 (40-60 minutes)

Harris Motocycles Ltd.

Harris Motorcycles Ltd. ("HML" or the company) is a public company whose shares are widely traded on several Canadian stock exchanges. The company, incorporated several years ago under the Canada Business Corporations Act, manufactures motorcycles which it markets through a large network of independent dealers across Canada. HML has a large bank loan outstanding, secured by inventories and accounts receivable.

The date is December 31, 19x5, and the company's staff has just completed taking a year end physical inventory of motorcycles. Each year HML schedules its production so that no raw materials or work in process are on hand by year end. A summary list is as follows:

Physical inventory on hand at close of business

Model	Year of Manufacture	Units on hand	Manufactured unit cost	Most recent selling price	Number of units sold during 19x5
500cc	19x5	200	$800	$1,200	800
500cc	19x4	160	$600	$ 700	120
500cc	19x3	80	$400	$ 350	4

The company's Controller has prepared a set of draft financial statements which he shows to the Vice-President of Finance. A portion of these statements reads as follows:

Current assets		
Cash	$	XXX
Accounts receivable, net		XXX
Inventory of motorcycles, at cost		288,000

Required:

Assume the role of the Vice-President of Finance. Evaluate the various alternative costing methods available to the company. Which do you recommend? Why? Assume that the financial statements are audited each year and must therefore be prepared in accordance with generally accepted accounting principles.

A Solution

The following is only one possible response to Problem 3. Different assumptions can be made when data is missing; this would change the response.

1. Objectives of accounting information appear to be to facilitate:

   a. Stewardship reporting to public shareholders, in compliance with generally accepted accounting principles, the Canada Business Corporations Act, any regulations of securities commissions, and other constraints.

   b. Loan decision by creditors (Hence, information might be needed on short term cash flows and the effect of inventory on the flows. However, such might be provided by a special purpose report for creditors).

   c. Prediction by shareholders (Hence, information might be needed on the long term cash flow potential and income of the company.)

   d. Possibly, evaluation of management performance by shareholders would be important; but, because no bonus based on net income is mentioned and there are no other references to this objective in the case we should not jump to conclusions.

    e. Possibly, postponement of income taxes is a consideration, but would be of less importance than the above.

2. <u>Identification</u> of accounting problems, ranked in order of importance:

    a. Select a suitable definition of "cost" (LIFO, FIFO, etc.)

    b. Select a definition of "market" replacement cost, etc.)

    c. Consider the lower of cost or market effects.

3. <u>Analysis</u> of accounting problems:

<u>Problem a</u>: Remember that generally accepted accounting principles (hereafter, "GAAP") are a constraint; therefore, we should consider only the stewardship methods outlined in Chapter 8 of the text. Choices include:

i.	Specific identification	iii.	FIFO
ii.	Weighted average	iv.	LIFO

Which method is suggested by an examination of the facts? Serial numbers exist for each motorcycle. Hence, specific identification is a possibility. Records can be kept, perhaps by year and model, of actual costs of manufacture. Can we assume that all 500 CC models made in 19x5 cost the same to manufacture? This might be a reasonable assumption for this case, but is probably unrealistic for real life.

When costs are identical as opposed to varying for the same model year, there is less chance of income manipulation with specific identification method. The auditors would probably not object to specific identification when income cannot be altered by selling one identical item instead of another. Thus, with our assumption about identical costs, specific identification is a possibility for inventory valuation purposes. However, if we assumed instead that manufacturing costs varied significantly for each model year, specific identification could meet with objections from auditors.

Weighted average is a possibility as well. But, it would have to be applied as a weighting of each model year. We could not sensibly compute a weighted average inventory cost for all model years because the costs vary too much. Weighted average can make sense in a factual situation where costs rise and fall. In a real situation, we would have to check the facts; in a classroom case we make a logical assumption based on available information. We might, for example, assume a period of rising manufacturing costs, (something which is indicated in the dollar amounts in the case) in which situation weighted average costing would likely not be as sensible as FIFO or LIFO.

FIFO would not make sense if we tried to combine all of the model years. It would be highly questionable, for instance, to sell a

19x5 model and charge cost of goods sold for a 19x3 model. We could, however, apply FIFO within each model year if, in a period of rising manufacturing costs, we wanted a higher inventory valuation on the balance sheet than would be provided by the other cost methods. Naive creditors or investors might prefer FIFO.

Whereas specific identification, weighted average and FIFO can be used for income tax purposes, LIFO cannot. Although the income tax objective was listed as a less important accounting objective for the company, it cannot be forgotten. If LIFO were chosen for external reporting purposes, it would be necessary to have a second set of inventory records in order to prepare information for income tax purposes. This could be costly. Consequently, LIFO would not be a wise choice unless officials of the company wanted an income figure which more closely reflected current costs than is possible with FIFO, weighted average and specific identification.

In summary, with an open-ended question like this one, where data and facts are missing, assumptions about the preparers and users interests and facts about the situation become essential. For example, how stable are manufacturing costs within each model year?

Consistency in the application of "GAAP" is another important issue. What method is HML presently using? The case does not say. Assumptions are required. The physical inventory listing would seem to suggest HML is using one cost for each model-year. Specific identification may be the most logical assumption, but others are possible. If a change in accounting principle is required, this involves some extra accounting in the year of change.

Problem b: Candidates for a definition of "market" in applying the lower of cost and market rule include:

i. Net realizable value ("NRV")
ii. Replacement cost to manufacture ("RC")

Which definition is suggested by the facts? The 19x4 500 CC models are no longer made. They are last year's model. The same applies for 19x3 500 CC models. Replacement cost to manufacture therefore makes no sense here. The cost to make a 19x5 500 CC has no bearing on 19x4 and 19x3 models.

Which definition is suggested by our objectives? Stewardship permits both NRV and RC. The banker is most interested in cash inflows if the motorcycles must be seized in the event that loan payments get behind schedule. Hence, net realizable value makes sense.

Problem c: Let us apply the lower of cost or market rule, since we have a definition of "cost" and "market". Our chosen method could be summarized as the "lower of specific identification cost and net realizable value." This would be disclosed in an accounting policy note to the financial statements, since a choice exists and users will want to appraise the wisdom of this choice. Using this rule, the financial statement disclosure might be as follows:

Current assets
    Cash $ XXX
    Accounts receivable, net   XXX

Inventory of motorcycles, at the lower of
  specific cost and net realizable value:

19x5 models on hand, at cost	$160,000	
19x4 models on hand, at cost	96,000	
19x3 models on hand, at net realizable value	28,000	284,000

Notice how our segregated disclosure helps investors and creditors who want to predict the effect of inventory transactions more so than one lump sum figure of $284,000. The separate disclosure warns investors that there is $96,000 of one-year-old stock on hand.

Will these be sold at 19x5 profit margins? Probably not. They will likely be sold at reduced profit margins. The investor can make an intelligent guess. The separate disclosure warns creditors that there is dated stock and tells them that, if inventory was sold at December 31, 19x5, they might expect to get at least $284,000 in cash inflow to cover their loan.

Incidentally, the entry to record the necessary write-down is:

Cost of goods sold*	$4,000	
Inventory of 19x3 500 CC motorcycles		$4,000

To record the write-down to net realizable values.

*An unusually large write-down might warrant separate disclosure on the income statement, to alert readers in accordance with the full disclosure concept.

4. <u>Recommendations</u> (The problems are referred to as a., b., and c., as previously indicated.)

  a. Define cost as that specifically identified for a model and year, since this is practical and best suits the facts. (Other recommendations are possible, if supported logically.)

  b. Define market as net realizable value, since this best facilitates the needs of creditors who want to appraise the cash inflow potential of inventories, which forms part of the security underlying their loan.

  c. Apply the "lower of specific cost and NRV" to inventories and recognize a $4,000 write-down. This is assumed to be consistent with the accounting policies of previous years. Hence, there is no consistency problem requiring disclosure in the company's financial statements. Separate disclosure of inventory by model and year is recommended to facilitate the prediction objective of investors and creditors.

9

Long-Lived Assets

Some long-lived assets, such as land, have an indefinite life whereas others, such as equipment, have a limited and estimable life. The long-lived assets with limited and estimable life may have a physical life longer than the time they are actually used, since they eventually become uneconomic to operate. A newer asset may be invented that has cheaper operating costs and that produces a more marketable product, rendering the older asset less economic, or nearly obsolete.

ROLE OF OBJECTIVES AND FACTS

The accounting treatment of long-lived assets must be viewed in terms of our objectives of accounting and facts. Under stewardship accounting, where the matching concept is highly important, emphasis is placed on trying to match the cost of depreciable assets to the revenue generated by these depreciable assets. Under other objectives, matching of depreciable asset costs may be far less important.

In government accounting, for instance, there is no or little need to ascertain an income figure. Governments do not exist to make a profit. Governments usually do not depreciate long-lived assets. (See C5-5 on page 235 of the textbook.) Their "revenue" comes from taxes, and they tax citizens at rates which, among other considerations, pay for the current year's interest expense -- which they incur on their borrowings made to acquire long-lived assets. Having taxed enough in order to make interest payments, they cannot also tax citizens when the assets depreciate, because to do so would be to double tax or count twice. For example, suppose that $1,000,000 is borrowed at 20% interest per annum to acquire an asset which lasts five years. In the first year, double counting would occur if both interest expense of $200,000 and depreciation expense of $200,000 were charged.

We have already seen, from Chapter 6, that those who are interested in the prediction objective tend to focus on cash flows. Depreciation is not a cash flow item. Hence, when predictions are needed of the *annual* flows from regular operations or operating results (as reflected on the income statement), accrual accounting income figures must be adjusted so as to delete the non-cash items.

In order to provide information for the income tax objective of accounting, the depreciation policies established by Revenue Canada have to be followed. These are described commencing on page 395 of the textbook.

When facts are not clear, the preparer has a greater opportunity to modify accounting treatment in order to facilitate the pursuit of one objective of accounting over another. Facts are often not clear in the two situations below:

1. Determining the useful economic life of a depreciable asset.

2. Ascertaining whether an expenditure (not an expense) constitutes a repair expense or an improvement (betterment) which ought to be capitalized.

Under a stewardship objective of accounting and in situation 1., the personality of the accountant comes into focus. Accordingly, depreciation expense and net income could vary widely, depending on the particular accountant's selection of one economic life over another.

Situation 2. applies to more than a stewardship objective. Income tax liabilities (which are based on taxable income) may be altered by expensing instead of capitalizing a cash outlay; expensing in effect both repairs and improves a depreciable long-lived asset. For instance, a faulty component in a manufacturing unit might be replaced with a part which reduces power expense and time required for weekly maintenance.

For stewardship purposes, what does a "conservative" accountant do, capitalize or expense the replacement part? If the accountant expenses the part, this year's income and retained earnings will be lower than if capitalization occurred. However, future years' income will be higher, since depreciation on the replacement part does not exist because there is no additional cost to depreciate. Conservatism in one year results in the opposite effect in succeeding years.

Which of capitalization or expensing is the most sensible accounting treatment for those who want to predict? Before we respond, we must consider both the user and preparer viewpoints. For instance, what obligation does the preparer have to cater to those who want to predict? The preparer may be concerned with potential legal liability (the chance of being sued by users), costs of accounting and reporting, legal requirements of reporting, and other factors. Hence, the preparer may not wish to prepare financial reports which are useful or understandable to someone who wishes to predict. However, if the preparer wishes to provide information which is useful for the prediction objective, two factors must be reported: (1) the *amount*, and (2) the *nature* of the expenditure. That is, the fact that the expenditure is not clearly an annual cash flow or a long-lived asset should be communicated. With such information and a knowledge of the amounts involved, the user can handle the transaction in the way he wants, in order to use the discounting model described in Chapter 6.

In summary, students should avoid seeking the one accounting treatment for fixed assets that they think would fit any set of objectives, facts, and constraints. Stewardship accounting is commonly used in Canada, and it requires use of the matching concept described in Chapter 5. However, other user needs exist, and they may be best served by quite different accounting measurement and disclosure.

TEXTBOOK *9-1: A SOLUTION (15-25 minutes)

Textbook question 9-1 examines the long-lived assets theme and attempts to tie together some of the various topics in Chapter 9. The quotation in the textbook is designed to remind students that (1) stewardship accounting is only one of several possible objectives of financial accounting, and (2) "facts" are often difficult to interpret, thereby causing problems in any attempt to cater to a particular objective or purpose of accounting.

Some companies have only one objective or purpose of financial accounting. For example, there is the owner-managed store that needs information only for income tax purposes. In this situation, the owner would probably try to minimize annual income. He would try to view situations where the facts are not clear in terms of minimizing annual income, thereby minimizing annual income tax payments.

Other companies may have two or more objectives or purposes of financial accounting. When facts are definite -- e.g., an uninsured depreciable asset has been totally destroyed in a fire -- objectives take on less significance. That is, a loss has occurred and we account for it as a loss. Even when the facts are definite, objectives of accounting may not be totally ignored. For example, when a preparer wishes to cater to the user interested in cash flow prediction, extra disclosure -- e.g., that the asset was uninsured and was destroyed on a particular date -- may be provided. When the date of the loss is known, it is easier to understand how much of the period's income was lowered because of the fire and because of the absence of the depreciable asset. In contrast, under a stewardship objective, the extra disclosure is not required by law and probably would not be provided. The accounting loss from the fire (shown on the income statement) would be the same under the stewardship and prediction objectives; but the amount of additional disclosure in notes to the financial statements would differ.

In summary, in circumstances where a company has more than one objective, it is necessary to order the objectives in importance. If stewardship is regarded as far more important than prediction, the extra disclosure about the fire probably would not be provided. When facts are not clear, the preparer must give even greater attention to the organization's objectives of accounting and to the question of which have priority.

The second part of the question asks for examples. Some are:

1. Capitalize an expenditure as a betterment? Or expense it as maintenance and repairs?

2. Which depreciation, depletion method or amortization method, should be used? What salvage value should be assumed? What rate or life should be chosen?

3. When should a long-lived asset be written down? At the date when the amount can be estimated or later?

4. Some aspects of research and development costs can lead to capitalization or expensing. (See page 414 of the textbook.)

5. Intangible drilling costs could be treated as expenses or assets.

6. Some costs of acquiring an asset (freight, or installation) might be capitalized or expensed.

7. Revisions to depreciation, depletion and amortization might occur as a result of hindsight or new information. Some adjustments might be made to prior years whereas others might be to future years.

For all of the above, vagueness in facts could be a sufficient reason for deciding either to capitalize or to expense the amount. The choice would be dependent on the prime objective of the preparer of the financial statements.

EXAMPLE 1

Some students have difficulty with journal entries which arise on the disposal or trade-in of a depreciable asset. Distinguishing cash flows from losses or gains is important, especially for prediction purposes, but also for complying with stewardship accounting as described in Chapter 14. Let us illustrate the mechanics before proceeding.

Suppose that an asset costing $10,000 upon which $7,225 of depreciation has accumulated:

Situation A: is sold for $2,000 cash.

Situation B: is traded in on a new asset. The new asset sells without a trade-in for $15,500 cash. The old asset was considered to be worth $2,500 as long as the seller also received a cheque for $13,500 on delivery of the new asset.

Solution to Situation A

The journal entry on disposal of the asset is:

Cash (asset +)	$2,000	
Accumulated depreciation (asset contra -)	7,225	
Loss on disposal (expense or loss +)	775	
Asset		$10,000
To record sale of long-lived asset.		

The "loss on disposal" account is the balancing figure; we know three of the account balances (cash; accumulated depreciation; asset), therefore, the loss or gain is the remainder.

Observe that the cash flow figure is $2,000. In a sense this is a scrap or residual value; it is not an annual cash flow. Hence, if we wanted to see what yield the asset produced over its lifetime, the $2,000 would be present valued (per Chapter 6) and deducted from the initial cost of $10,000. The net figure ($10,000 less present value of $2,000) would be compared to the annual net cash flows received from the asset. If the asset were a taxi, annual net cash flows would consist of taxi fares less gas, oil, licenses, insurance, salary to the driver, and other cash outlays, except interest and principal on any funds borrowed to acquire the taxi.

Solution to Situation B

The trick in situation B is to determine the fair market value of the old asset at the date of trade-in. The calculation is:

Cash selling price of new asset with no trade-in	$15,500
Cash selling price with trade-in	13,500
Difference, which represents value of trade-in	$ 2,000

The $2,500 figure noted in the question is artificial or sales gimmickry. A salesperson is trying to get the customer to focus on the trade-in and not on the cash payment of $13,500. The important point is that the new asset costs $15,000 when there is no trade-in. The journal entry to record disposal of the old asset and acquisition of the new one would be:

Asset (new)	$15,500	
Accumulated depreciation (old)	7,225	
Loss on disposal of old asset	775	
Asset (old)		$10,000
Cash		13,500

The "loss on disposal" remains as in Situation A.

System Design

At some point in our studies of an accounting course, attention must be given to choosing accounting principles for a new organization. Such a focus enables us to better evaluate alternatives. Problem 1 tests an understanding of long-lived asset valuation principles.

NEW PROBLEM 1 (20-40 minutes)

T. Gilbert Ltd. (the company) was incorporated on January 1, 19x1 for the purpose of operating a bus service between a city and an out-of-town construction site. Construction is expected to take five years and one bus capable of transporting 40 workers is all that is needed by the company. At the end of five years, the company will be wound up and the assets liquidated.

A contract has been signed with the main contractor at the site guaranteeing revenue of $80,000 per year for the five years. The construction company will pay for all gas, oil, and repair costs. T. Gilbert has to supply drivers, and has estimated the cost of this at $25,000 per annum. The bus will cost $225,000 and has an estimated salvage value at the end of five years of $25,000.

Required:

Choose an appropriate depreciation accounting method or policy for the company and explain why you have selected it. Income tax effects may be ignored. Assumptions are required.

A Solution

Problem 1 might be regarded as a less directed case. Some assumptions have to be made about the interests of the preparer and user and the objectives of financial accounting. Otherwise, the choice of depreciation policies cannot be defended.

What are some logical objectives of financial accounting for this company? Presumably we can ignore the income tax objective, although the question is not entirely clear on this point. The owners may want stewardship financial statements for each year. Possibly a bank will loan some of the $225,000 purchase price. If so, it may want either a stewardship report or one which helps in the assessment of management, or in prediction.

If a stewardship report is desired and the preparer wishes to choose the simplest possible depreciation method, a straight line charge of $40,000 per year would suffice:

$$\frac{\$225,000 - \$25,000}{5 \text{ years}} = \$40,000 \text{ per year.}$$

This would result in an income statement with revenue of $80,000 and expenses of $65,000 ($40,000 depreciation plus $25,000 of drivers' salaries) per year for a net income of $15,000 annually.

For a simple stewardship purpose, such an income statement would be adequate. However, is it sensible to show a stable income of $15,000 per year?

Before we can respond to this question let us compute the yield or return on investment which is generated by the investment of $225,000. After all, if we know the yield we know what the owner(s) of T. Gilbert Ltd. were expecting when they formed their company. Quite possibly they would not have formed the company unless they could get a satisfactory yield on their investment.

For simplicity let us assume that the entire $225,000 is equity of one owner, Mr. Gilbert. (Other assumptions would not affect the overall yield to the company. However, they could affect the separate yield on equity and debt if some funds were borrowed.) By a process of trial and error, we can determine that the yield approximates 10%:

	Present Value
Present value of $55,000 ($80,000 - $25,000) received at the *end* of each of the next five years:	
$55,000 x 3.798 (page 761 of the textbook)	$208,890
Present value of investment:	
Initial outlay	$225,000
Less scrap value of $25,000:	
$25,000 x .6209 (page 757 of the textbook)	$ 15,523
	$209,477

Although the $209,477 does not equal the $208,890, the figures are close enough for our purposes. With a yield of 10% in each year the amortization of the $225,000 investment in cash would look like this for the first three years:

Initial outlay	$225,000
Interest at 10% for first year (i.e., income)	22,500
	247,500
Cash received at end of first year ($80,000 - $25,000)	55,000
Capital at beginning of second year	192,500
Interest at 10% for second year (i.e., income)	19,250
	173,250
Cash received at end of second year	55,000
Capital at beginning of third year	118,250
Interest at 10% for third year (i.e., income)	11,825
	130,075
Cash received at end of third year	55,000
	75,075

If depreciation expense were chosen in a varying amount, so that each of the five years would show an income that coincides with a 10% return on investment, the income statements would appear as follows:

	Income Statements		
	19x1	19x2	19x3
Revenue	$ 80,000	$ 80,000	$ 80,000
Drivers' salaries	25,000	25,000	25,000
Depreciation expense	32,500	35,750	43,175
	57,500	60,750	68,175
Income (ignoring income tax)	$ 22,500	$ 19,250	$ 11,825
Investment outstanding in year	$225,000	$192,500	$118,250
Return on investment (income divided by investment)	10%	10%	10%

In contrast, when straight-line depreciation of $40,000 per year is used, the income each year is $15,000 per year. This results in an income figure which shows an increasing return on investment as the asset gets older:

	Investment	Income	Return on Investment
19x1	$225,000	$15,000	6.67%
19x2	192,500	15,000	7.79%
19x3	118,250	15,000	12.69%

Does the increasing yield make sense? If our purpose in reporting is to provide information for those who wish to evaluate management, the straight-line depreciation basis causes misleading results. Management made *one* decision with respect to acquiring the bus, a decision which locked them in for five years. Doesn't it make sense for purposes of evaluating management to show a constant yield of 10% per year over this time?

If the objective of financial accounting is prediction, maybe an income statement is not required in this situation. If persons know about the $80,000 and $25,000 figures, and about the $225,000 and $25,000 scrap, they have all the information they need. Depreciation policy is not relevant to them.

10 *Liabilities and Related Expenses*

The liability side of the balance sheet has recently experienced and will continue to experience significant changes, as accountants and users attempt to clarify the definition of a liability. In earlier chapters,* we saw some clear situations where neither party to a transaction had yet performed the required services; in such a case, the eventual receiver of the service did not record a liability until the service was performed. For example, a contract (which accountants label as an "executory contract") may have been signed between a hockey player and a team whereby $200,000 was to be paid to the player per season for five years. When should the hockey team record a liability?

For many years accountants have recorded a liability in the above circumstances when a service was performed. If the player was paid weekly, in theory the liability would accrue each day as service was provided and be decreased as cash payment was made to the player. By doing this type of record-keeping, accountants were following the matching concept. Income measurement was stressed; and the balance sheet was relegated to being a collection of assets and liabilities needed to balance cash flows of the past and income statement accruals.

Some users, such as those interested in cash flow prediction, felt that this type of balance sheet was not living up to its potential. They reasoned that commitments to pay cash flows in the future, such as those for the hockey player, should be disclosed. If disclosure did not occur directly on the balance sheet, they felt that certain transactions affecting the future should be described in notes to the financial statements.

In order to accomodate different users, accountants have begun a process of changing the definition of a liability. This chapter shows the current

---

*Page 44 of the textbook, for example.

unsettled state of affairs. Leases, which are in essence purchases of
assets, are shown as a liability. The liability is offset by an asset,
such as "equipment under lease." Other leases are not shown as a liability, but some note that disclosure is provided. Some aspects of income
taxation and its effects on the future are treated as a form of liabilities. But the liability, unlike the treatment given to some leases, is
not discounted for interest effects. Pension accounting is quite unsettled and inadequate and its complications are beyond the level of an
introductory class.

What prime message should you derive from the chapter and this discussion?
Prepare yourself for change if you expect to encounter financial statements at some future date. Keep abreast of current developments before
you prepare or use a financial statement. Changes in the accounting rules
can significantly affect income measurement and balance sheet disclosure.
Accounting will change to meet the changing business practices and
conditions.

TEXTBOOK *10-14: A SOLUTION (15-25 minutes)

This problem should not be attempted until you have thoroughly read and
throught about the various topics discussed in the chapter. Your
understanding of the subject of accounting will be greatly improved by
putting yourself in the position of a reader of financial statements
and asking what you would need to judge the "soundness" of a company.
For example, if you were a banker being asked to lend a company
$1,000,000, what would you want to know about its "liabilities"?
Suppose that it had signed "contracts" to (1) provide pensions to its
employees, (2) lease equipment over a 10 year period, (3) repay a mortgage on its building, and (4) pay higher income taxes in the future
because its income tax depreciation (capital cost allowance) has been
used up. Which of these would concern your? Are they liabilities or
executory contracts, or both in parts?

Cash prediction may be easier for some users with disclosure than with
current methods of measurement. For example, income tax effects of
claiming varying amounts of capital cost allowance occur. At some
future date, when little capital cost allowance is available, income
tax payments get larger. Disclosure of the amounts of capital cost
allowance available and of the time when they might be used would help
in estimating cash outflows for income tax purposes. Current practice
does not require such information; instead all it does is compute
timing differences between depreciation and capital cost allowance and
multiply this by the current income tax rate. No discounting occurs.

In lease accounting where the asset under lease is not shown as an asset,
with a corresponding liability, there often is only disclosure of the
next five or so years' lease payments instead of over the lifetime of the
lease. When leases are capitalized, disclosure of lease payments beyond
five or so years may be inadequate for prediction of long term cash
effects. In order to capitalize, a discount rate is assumed. Maybe a
user feels that a different rate is more appropriate for his/her

circumstances instead of the rate used by the accountant.

Funding (cash outflow) of pension plans is often at odds with the expensing of pension costs. Disclosure of cash outflows would help investors know how much cash is leaving the company and how much is being retained for investment elsewhere. See page 462 of the textbook. Maybe management is paying too much into low yield pension assets when it could be investing in lucrative projects. The cash versus accrual differences of pension plan accounting are not minor because there could be long time periods between expensing and cash funding. Present measurement rules provide little information on cash funding, and it is the latter which those interested in prediction need.

Accountants have been preoccupied with measurement because of the two "original" objectives of accounting: stewardship and income tax. Both tend to be tied to matching. A shift away from a nearly 100% focus on measurement has been occurring as other objectives of accounting have taken on significance. People are realizing that there is not one all-purpose measurement. Biases occur in measurement, and so forth.

INCOME TAX ALLOCATION

The textbook stresses (page 453) the point that an asset which has *no* capital cost allowance (CCA) left to be claimed for income tax purposes is worth *less* than one which has CCA available. The accounting measurement and disclosure question is how to report this fact in financial statements.

At the present time in Canada, accountants employ the deferral method of tax allocation. Many people find this approach confusing. It is based on matching, per Chapter 5, and the balance sheet is relegated to "second class" status of showing the offsetting debit or credit to successive attempts at matching.

Using a depreciable asset as an example, when CCA exceeds depreciation, the tax allocation portion of the income tax expense journal entry is:

    Income tax expense $XXX
        Deferred income tax $XXX

When depreciation exceeds CCA the journal entry is:

    Deferred income tax $XXX
        Income tax expense $XXX

Both of these are *non-cash* journal entries.

Unless management of a company is weak, it will claim maximum CCA in order to lower its income tax liability and corresponding cash outflow. Income tax allocation accounting is unrelated to management's decision to claim maximum CCA. What tax allocation accounting accomplishes is primarily to send out a *signal*. This *signal* says little more than that at some time in the future, CCA will be decreasing, and higher cash outflows will occur to pay income taxes. We do not know *when* the "additional" cash flow is needed, nor do we know *how much* is needed. Deferred income tax is not a liability in the same way bonds payable are.

Let us now do a deferred income tax problem. It contains some simplifications, and in that sense is not representative of how complex these tax allocation situations can become. We have purposely kept the problem to "basics" because of the difficulties many people have with the topic.

NEW PROBLEM 1 (30-50 minutes)

The following information relates to A. Stawinoga Ltd.:

	Year ended December 31	
	19x1	19x2
Income before depreciation and income tax	$100,000	$20,000
Depreciation	30,000	30,000
Capital cost allowance	60,000	20,000
Income tax rate	40%	40%

Required:

Provide income tax journal entries for 19x1 and 19x2.

A Solution

Various techniques may be used to compute the figures needed. The following one is useful for a variety of tax allocation problems. It consists of setting up three columns: one for the income statement effect; a second for timing differences between CCA and depreciation; and a third for balance sheet effects. Year 19x1 would be handled this way:

	Income Statement	Timing Difference	Balance Sheet
Income before depreciation and income tax	$100,000	$	$(100,000)
Depreciation	(30,000)	30,000	
Capital cost allowance		(60,000)	60,000
	$ 70,000	$(30,000)	$ (40,000)
Income tax effect at 40%	$ 28,000	$(12,000)	$ (16,000)

- 132 -

The brackets are placed around credits or reductions. For example, the $100,000 under "balance sheet" has brackets because it represents a potential income tax *liability*. If there were no CCA, 40% of $100,000 would be a payable (which is a credit). Depreciation of $30,000 under the income statement has a credit because it *reduces* the $100,000 debt, leaving $70,000 at a 40% tax rate as a debit to income tax expense. The $60,000 under timing differences is a credit because, in the absence of tax depreciation, $60,000 at 40% would be credited to deferred income tax.

The technique helps to reduce clerical errors. Each line must cross balance: the figures without brackets must equal the figures with brackets. The totals also cross add. The journal entry for 19x1 would be:

Income tax expense	$28,000	
Deferred income tax		$12,000
Income tax payable		16,000

The figures for 19x2 are:

	Income Statement	Timing Difference	Balance Sheet
Income before depreciation and income tax	$ 20,000	$	$(20,000)
Depreciation	(30,000)	30,000	
Capital cost allowance		(20,000)	20,000
	$(10,000)	$ 10,000	$ 0
Income tax effect at 40%	$ (4,000)	$ 4,000	$ 0

The journal entry for 19x2 is:

Deferred income tax	$ 4,000	
Income tax recovery (income statement credit)		$ 4,000

The $4,000 income tax credit would appear on the partial income statement as follows:

Income before depreciation and income tax	$ 20,000
Depreciation expense	(30,000)
Loss before income tax recovery	(10,000)
Income tax recovery	4,000
Net loss	$ 6,000

LEASES

The growth of leasing in Canada can be attributed to several factors; but two prominent ones for our purposes are income tax law and financial disclosure. Income tax law has been tightened now, but at one time it gave lessors such favourable tax benefits through CCA that they were able to make good returns on investments by borrowing funds and also giving lessees attractive payments and rates. Chapter 6 indicated that the closer cash flows are to the present time, the higher their worth. CCA reduces income tax, thereby increasing *net* cash inflows from a lease contract. The increase occurs in early years when maximum CCA can be claimed. In some situations, a lessor could use the CCA to offset profits from other unrelated parts of the business, perhaps from manufacturing activities. Overall, the high yield encouraged lessors to expand their operations.

Lessees were able, through most of the 1970s, to avoid showing leased assets as "liabilities." A naive lender who calculated debt to equity ratios (see page 684 of the textbook) to see how much equity protection was offered for the debt might have ignored leased assets and obligations for lease payments. This hope, that lenders were naive, seems to have encouraged lessees to sign lease contracts.

Accountants were forced by public concern to respond to the change in business practice of leasing instead of borrowing. They decided to require capitalization by the lessee of those leases which in substance were really purchases of an asset.

Problem 2, below, illustrates the accounting journal entires for a lessee who has, in substance, acquired an asset. Textbook pages 448-451 should be read thoroughly before attempting Problem 2.

NEW PROBLEM 2 (15-25 minutes)

R. Long Ltd. has leased an asset for 10 years. Lease payments of $15,000 per year are due at the end of each of the ten years, and a 10% rate of interest is considered appropriate. The asset is to be depreciated over 12 years on a straight-line basis; it can be acquired for $1 at the end of 10 years. According to Canadian GAAP, the lease ought to be capitalized.

Required:

Prepare journal entries to record:

a. the capital lease on R. Long Ltd.'s books;
b. the first lease payment of $15,000;
c. depreciation expense for the year.

A Solution

The capitalized value of the lease, according to Table 4 on page 761 of the textbook, is:

$$\$15,000 \times 6.1446 = \underline{\$92,169}$$

The journal entry to record capitalization of the lease is:

a. Equipment held under lease $92,169
       Present value of lease obligation $92,169

The first lease payment would be recorded as:

b. Interest expense (10% x $92,169) $ 9,217
       Present value of lease obligations   5,783
       Cash $15,000

Depreciation per year is:

Depreciation expense $ 7,681
   Equipment held under lease –
     accumulated depreciation $ 7,681

The balance sheet presentation by the lessee at the end of the first year would be:

Assets

Long-lived assets:
   Equipment held under lease $92,169
   Less accumulated depreciation   7,681
                                                  $84,488

Liabilities

Present value of lease obligation $86,386

The asset and liability amounts do not agree because the liability is being amortized over 10 years on a present value basis, and the leased asset is being depreciated over 12 years on a straight-line basis.

11 *Capital Accounts, I*

Chapters 11 and 12 devote considerable space to constraints imposed on shareholders' equity accounts by corporate law, and other restrictions required by the *CICA Handbook*. Often these constraints exist in order to protect creditors, or to shield naive investors from a few less-than-honest individuals or companies. It is helpful in approaching our study of these chapters to recognize that the requirements may represent "over-kill" or excessive protection. Nevertheless, in order to understand financial accounting based on a stewardship objective, we must be aware of the types of restrictions which exist so that we can fairly interpret financial statements. In time, the constraints will change, as business practices and other factors change. For example, current laws affecting the legal liability of auditors encourage them to publish restrictions in the *CICA Handbook* which reduce the possibility of income manipulation by their clients. A change in the laws will result in a change in constraints.

We will have to resort to memorization for much of Chapter 11 and about two-thirds of Chapter 12. The remainder of Chapter 12 introduces pre-sentations which may be helpful for other objectives or purposes of financial accounting, such as evaluation of management by outsiders, and facilitating cash flow prediction.

The first question is from the textbook, 11-2, and is conceptual in nature. It is followed by a "how-to-do-it" so that the conceptual and procedural may be linked.

TEXTBOOK *11-2 (20-30 minutes)

"At times, constraints or rules overpower the importance of objectives and facts because the constraints have the weight of law behind them" (page 485 of the textbook).

Examples where legislation might govern the method of accounting or the form of disclosure are as follows:

a. Method of accounting (mainly for limited companies):

   i. There is a distinction in corporate law between retained earnings
       and "capital" contributed by owners. The latter is regarded as
       protection for creditors in the event of losses or liquidation.
       Creditors have a right to insist that they be paid before owners
       can withdraw their original invested capital. Creditors loan
       money to the entity with this assumption of protection in mind.
       Hence, they would be very unhappy to discover that the entity had
       declared dividends out of original invested capital. The creditors
       might sue the directors of the company for declaring such a divi-
       dend. Some large creditors even have the power to inssist that
       the company not pay dividends over a certain amount and thereby
       lower retained earnings. This is an example of a restrictive debt
       covenant, which is usually written into the legal contract at the
       time the debt is issued.

       This distinction in law carries over to accounting because the law
       specifies the content of some parts of financial statements.
       Dividends must be separately disclosed in the financial statements,
       so that creditors and others (e.g., income tax officials) can see
       how much the owners are taking out of the business.

  ii. Partly related to i., there is a distinction in accounting and in
       income tax between expenditures relating to "capital" or owners'
       capital, and expenses incurred to earn "income." Decades ago
       (before 1917) stewardship was perhaps the only objective of
       financial accounting. The purpose of financial statements was to
       tell shareholders how much net income was legally available for a
       dividend. Hence, distinctions between what was "capital" and
       what was "a return on capital," or income, were critical. This
       concern has survived and is still with us today. For example,
       accountants typically treat legal fees and other expenditures for
       a share (not bond) issue as capital (or owners' capital) transac-
       tions. There are many other examples, and you will see them
       throughout courses in accounting.

 iii. For those legal jurisdictions which still have par value shares,
       the distinction between par value and contributed surplus must
       be made in the accounts. Dividends may be declared and debited
       to contributed surplus more readily than they can be debited to
       common share capital. Disclosure of such dividends is essential,
       and failure to disclose may be illegal under a variety of circum-
       stances.

b. Form of disclosure (mainly for limited companies):

   The various Provincial Companies Acts, and the Canada Business Corporations Act, require certain minimum disclosure in financial statements presented to shareholders. These are "stewardship reporting"
   requirements. That is, shareholders invest money and companies must,
   by law, give shareholders minimum information (feedback) in return.

Examples of such requirements for separate (not grouped) disclosure are:

i. Each type and amount of shares authorized and issued.

ii. Par values, if any. (This applies only in some provincial legislation.)

iii. Retained earnings.

iv. Amounts owing from or to officers and directors of the company, and material transaction with these people during the year.

v. Remuneration (salaries, bonuses, etc.) of all forms to directors and officers of the company.

vi. Net income for the year.

vii. Segment reporting if companies are diversified and exceed a certain size. (This is discussed in Chapter 12 of the textbook).

Problem 1, below, involves the winding up of a partnership and the creation of a new corporation. It stresses a journal entry approach, and hence is a good review. It also examines the need to record opening balances of a new entity at fair market values, rather than the old book values of the partnership, when ownership interest changes. In accordance with the entity concept noted in Chapter 5, a new entry has been created.

NEW PROBLEM 1 (40-60 minutes)

Chris and Mary are partners in a retail clothing boutique. After being in business several years, the two decide to federally incorporate (meaning under the Canada Business Corporations Act) their business as Oriole Boutique Ltd., effective January 1, 19x1. Chris and Mary share profits and losses in the partnership in a ratio of 1:1. Prior to winding up of the partnership and the subsequent incorporation, the balance sheet of the partnership indicated the following:

Assets

Current assets:		
Cash		$ 18,000
Inventory		125,000
Total current assets		143,000
Non current assets:		
Furniture and fixtures	$113,000	
Less accumulated depreciation	33,000	
Net furniture and fixtures		80,000
Total assets		$223,000

Liabilities and owners' equity

Current liabilities:
Accounts payable $ 9,000

Non current liabilities:
Note payable to Mary 20,000

Owners' equity:
Capital, Chris $97,000
Capital, Mary 97,000 194,000

Total liabilities and owners' equity $223,000

Prior to transferring the assets to the corporation, the partners decide to adjust the books of the partnership to reflect current replacement costs.

The inventory has a current replacement cost of $255,000; and the furniture and fixtures, $85,000 (replacement cost in used condition).

The new corporation was authorized to issue 100,000 common shares and 1,000 preferred shares, both without par value. Common shares were to be issued at a price of $10 per share and in proportion to the replacement cost of each person's contribution. In addition, common shares were to be issued to a friend, Drew, who agreed to invest $25,000 in the new corporation.

Mary chose to accept 1,000 preferred shares, without par value, for the note owed to her. Each share carries a fixed dividend rate of $2 per share per annum.

A lawyer was paid $5,000 for incorporating the new company.

Required:

a. Prepare journal entries to revalue the partnership, to transfer the assets to the new corporation in exchange for common and preferred shares, and to distribute the common and preferred shares to the partners.

b. Prepare journal entries to organize the new corporation.

c. Indicate the number of common shares each investor would receive.

d. Suppose the new investor, Drew, had wanted to appraise how well the partnership had performed while it was in business, before deciding to go into the new venture. Explain how the accounting treatment of the following might affect his appraisal:

   i. salary payments to Chris and Mary.
  ii. interest payments to Mary on the note owing to her.

A Solution

a. Journal entries required to close the partnership's books:

1.

Inventory	$130,000	
Capital, Chris		$65,000
Capital, Mary		$65,000
To write inventories up to current replacement cost.		

Students should note how the gain on writing up the inventories is credited directly to the capital accounts, in their income sharing ratios. Partnership accounts (which are not constrained by legislation affecting partnership), unlike limited companies, do not have to distinguish between original invested capital and retained earnings. Hence, there is normally just one line, "capital," on the balance sheet. However, there may be a separate statement of changes in partners' capital. The gain arises because inventories were carried at historic cost on the books, not at current replacement cost.

2.

Furniture and fixtures, cost	$ 5,000	
Capital, Chris		$ 2,500
Capital, Mary		$ 2,500
To write fixed assets up to current replacement cost.		

Notice how the gain is once again credited in equal proportions to Chris and Mary. Such a gain arises because current replacement cost in used condition exceeds net book value by $5,000.

3.

Common shares, Oriole Boutique Ltd.	$329,000	
Allowance for depreciation, furniture and fixtures	33,000	
Accounts payable	9,000	
Cash		$ 18,000
Inventory		225,000
Furniture and fixtures		118,000
To record the transfer of the assets to Oriole Boutique Ltd. in exchange for $329,000 (32,900 shares) of common.		

Students should note that the partnership has given up its net assets, so to speak in return for common shares in Oriole Boutique Ltd. ("OBL"). Think of the partnership as now having one asset, the shares in OBL, and the claims to this asset are the two partners' capital accounts.

We are now down to the following equation:

$$assets = owners' \text{ } equity$$

The $329,000 represents the fair value of the partnership as a whole which in this problem exactly equals the sum of the current replacement costs of the assets less liabilities. The new shareholder, Drew, would probably have to agree to this figure and to the current market values of assets and liabilities.

4.

Capital, Chris	$164,500	
Capital, Mary	164,500	
Common shares, Oriole Boutique Ltd.		$329,000

To wind up the partnership and distribute
the asset (shares in OBL) to the individual
partners.

b. To form the new corporation.

5.

Cash	$ 38,000	
Inventory	255,000	
Furniture and fixtures	85,000	
Organization costs, legal fees	5,000	
Accounts payable		$ 9,000
Note payable to Mary		20,000
Common shares, no par value		354,000

To record formation of a new corporation.

The cash figure is the $18,000 transferred from the partnership plus $25,000 invested by Drew less $5,000 paid in legal fees. Notice that accumulated depreciation on furniture and fixtures is not carried forward to the new corporation. The "cost" to the corporation is $85,000, representing current replacement cost. Organization costs are typically expensed at a later date against revenues when the amount involved is then not material (see Chapter 5). In theory, organization costs may not be revenue, but could be capital transactions (owners' capital transactions).

6.

Note payable to Mary	$ 20,000	
Preferred shares, no par value		$ 20,000

To record the cancellation of the note and
the issue of 1,000 preferred shares accepted
in exchange for the note.

For illustrative purposes, let us see what the new balance sheet of Oriole Boutique Ltd. looks like:

Oriole Boutique Ltd.

Balance Sheet

January 1, 19x1

Assets

Current assets:
Cash	$ 38,000
Inventory	255,000
Total current assets	293,000
Non current assets:	
Furniture and fixtures, at cost	85,000
Organization costs	5,000
Total assets	$383,000

Liabilities and Shareholders' Equity

Current liabilities:
Accounts payable	$ 9,000
Shareholders' equity:	
Preferred shares (no par value, 1,000 shares issued and outstanding)	20,000
Common shares (no par value, 100,000 shares authorized; 35,400 issued and outstanding)	354,000
Total liabilities and shareholders equity	$383,000

c. Common shares would be distributed as follows (number of shares):

Old partners:		
Chris	16,450	
Mary	16,450	32,900
New shareholder, Drew		2,500
Number of issued common shares		35,400

d. As explained in Chapter 11 of the text, a partnership has the option under generally accepted accounting principles of showing partners' salaries and interest either as an expense, or outside of the income statement (on a partners' capital statement) as distribution of income. The new shareholder, Drew, might want to look at the trend in net incomes of the partnership over several years, to appraise the prospects for the new corporation. But net income might be misleading either because:

i. Salaries and interest are included in the income statement as expenses. Also they may not be at fair market rates for equivalent work performed, or a fair interest rate. What if Chris and Mary had decided to pay themselves unrealistically large salaries each year? Then, in effect, some portion of the salary constitutes a distribution of net income (like a dividend for a limited company). The other portion represents money received for services, at fair value. How does Drew determine just what is net income and what is a withdrawal of net income? Judgment is required as to what a fair salary would be. In this case, he would add back to recorded net income the portion he feels is an effective distribution of net income; or

ii. Salaries and interest bypass the income statement and are shown in the Statement of Partners' Capital as distributions of net income. Some accountants choose this treatment because they feel such amounts, being non-arm's length, are too subjective to appear in the income statement. Drew's problem is once again to somehow adjust net income to reflect a fair charge for salaries and interest. In this case, he would deduct from recorded net income some figure for salaries and interest, so as to get a reasonable picture of recurring (or likely to be recurring) net income each year.

12 *Capital Accounts, II*

Chapter 12 in the textbook covers a variety of topics, many of them having important overtones for a prediction objective of accounting. Some topics also involve minor aspects of a stewardship purpose. For example, interim or quarterly financial statements, divisional reports, and forecast data clearly are designed to aid persons who are attempting to predict future operating results; the reports would not be needed solely for the steward-ship objective. The separation of transactions into

1. ordinary events,
2. unusual items,
3. extraordinary items,
4. prior period adjustments, and
5. capital transactions,

directly or indirectly, is an attempt to show which various business acti-vities are of a recurring nature and may repeat in the immediate future, and which are nonrecurring. As we have seen in Chapters 5 and 6, the worth of a business is the present value of future operating results (converted to a cash basis in order to permit discounting).

Some of the other topics, such as share options and warrants, and earnings per share, address the question of who is to benefit from the results of operations: the shareholders or creditors? Other subjects, such as con-tingencies and self-insurance costs, are handled in a manner which attempts to minimize income manipulation by a few managers. If manipulation can be reduced, then more credibility attaches to the operating result figures and trends. Observe, for instance, how the "conservatism" concept men-tioned in Chapter 5 has been redefined for purposes of recording contin-gencies ("future" expenses or losses). Ultra conservatism clearly is not permitted under contingency accounting constraints.

If manipulation can be minimized, the resulting financial reports might also prove useful in the evaluation of management by "outsiders" such as shareholders and creditors. When reading the chapter, notice the degree to which the constraints imposed by the *CICA Handbook* attempt to minimize income manipulation by preparers.

Most of the topics in Chapter 12 are far more complex than we have been able to show in an introductory textbook. A thorough reading of the chapter will, however, permit a user to be able to understand financial statements of many companies. We also do not have the space in *Self Study Problems* to deal with all of these topics.

We strongly recommend that you take the time to understand clearly the theoretical distinctions among the five transactions listed in the first paragraph of this chapter. The intention underlying the distinctions is to accomodate particular objectives of accounting. But in practice, it can be difficult to separate, for instance, an extraordinary transaction from an ordinary or recurring one, since facts may not be clear. Hence, from a user's viewpoint, it is important to remember that, although the definitions of these different transactions may exist in accounting books, implementation in practice may fall far short of the theory.

Example 1 and the solution to Textbook *12-10, below, address the earnings per share (EPS) statistics, instead of several other analytical statistics we might have chosen, mainly because EPS is widely publicized by financial analysts. We conclude this chapter with a case which reviews material from this and several of the previous chapters, in order to give students practice in integration of topics.

EXAMPLE 1:

Suppose that X Company Ltd. has earnings after income taxes of $100,000 for 19x1, and has 50,000 common shares outstanding. The company has a share option plan. Currently outstanding are 10,000 options which may be exercised for one common share per option at any time at $15 a share. The shares of X Company Ltd. are currently trading for $20. The company has, in the past, earned 10% on an after-tax basis on new investments.

Required:

It is the company's year end, and you are preparing earnings per share figures for disclosure on the income statement. Compute basic earnings per share and fully diluted earnings per share.

A Solution

	Shares outstanding	Earnings after income taxes	Earnings per share
Actual, at year end	50,000	$100,000	$2.00
Assumed exercise of all options would add	10,000	15,000	
	60,000	$115,000	$1.917

- 145 -

The 10,000 options, if exercised, would result in option holders giving the company (10,000 x $15) $150,000 in return for receiving 10,000 shares (e.g., debit cash for $150,000 and credit common shares for $150,000). With the $150,000 cash, the company can generate $15,000 additional earnings after income taxes ($150,000 x 10% which can be earned on new invesments). Exercise of all options would add 10,000 new shares and $15,000 of new earnings after income taxes.

Basic earnings per share is $2.00. It is the earnings or income after income taxes divided by the number of common shares outstanding. Each shareholder presumably earned $2.00 for every share held, even though the dividend per share may be much less than $2.00. Basic EPS tends to be a stewardship report on the past.

Fully diluted earnings per share is $1.917. It is a hypothetical earnings per share, one that would result *if* all option holders had exercised their options at the *beginning* of the year just completed. Fully diluted EPS indicates to existing shareholders what potential dilution (reduction) in their basic EPS would occur if all option holders switched to become shareholders. Hence, it may help shareholders predict their future earnings per share if all other factors are constant and the options are exercised. Of course, potential exercise is not the same as probably or likely exercise. Option holders will not switch until the market share price exceeds the option price of $15. If the market share price is $14, then no exercise will occur (it is cheaper to buy the share on the open market) and the "potential" exercise does not materialize. It is in this sense that we say that fully diluted earnings per share provides only a *rough* predictor of future earnings per share. In addition, net income next year may be quite different than net income of this year.

After this brief example, we are now in a position to discuss textbook question 12-10, which seeks to sensitize students to earnings per share concepts. Question 12-10 may take 10-20 minutes to answer thoroughly.

TEXTBOOK *12-10: A SOLUTION (10-20 minutes)

In calculating earnings per share, it is necessary to make assumptions (as we did in Example 1), in both practice and classroom situations, as to what a firm could earn with any cash received *if* the options were exercised. It would be misleading to take into account only the additional shares to be issued and to assume that the cash received from exercising the options did not generate any income. Such new cash would be invested in productive assets, and earnings presumably would increase. If recognition is to be given to the shares that *might* be issued, it must also be given to the increase in earnings that would result from their issuance. The assumption is an "opportunity cost" concept, which was discussed in Chapter 6 of the textbook.

The next problem, a case, deals in part with "barter" transactions and also with some of the events discussed in Chapter 12 which impact upon the owners' equity section of the balance sheet. It helps to review some course themes and the "how-to-do-it."

Media Ltd. (A Case)

Media Ltd. ("ML" or the company) operates several radio and television stations in Canada. The voting shares are closely held; however, the company has sold bonds to the general public across the country. As a result it requires audited annual financial statements because, in a sense, it is a publicly-owned company.

The controller of the company, Mr. Myers, is attempting to finalize the accounts and prepare financial statements for the year ended October 31, 19x9. He is presently having difficulty with the following transactions:

1. The company received a notice of reassessment from Revenue Canada in the amount of $100,000 which relates to the year ended 19x7. Mr.Myers has reviewed the assessment and is in agreement that the sum is owed by ML.

2. ML released a motion picture which it made in October, 19x9. Initial reviews were poor and there was uncertainty about the probable success of the film.

3. Approximately $200,000 at suggested retail price of advertising time was taken up by local newspapers under barter arrangements. These barter arrangements involved agreements with the newspapers to trade company advertising about the newspapers on the radio, for advertising about ML in the newspapers. In most circumstances, radio advertising about the newspapers occurred at times when no other advertisers had bought "commercial time" from the radio station.

4. The company paid $10,000 for an option to purchase property in a small town at a price of $1,000,000. The option expires October 31, 19x10.

5. The company renovated the interior of one of its radio stations. The renovation was initially conducted by idle radio station employees. Unfortunately, two weeks after the construction was completed, a ceiling fell in. As a result, ML a) had to hire a construction company to do the renovation again, and b) was being sued by a Rolling Stone fan who was injured when the ceiling fell in.

    The controller was considering capitalizing the following costs for the renovation: interest, labour cost for employees who worked on the project, overhead (such as heat, electricity and cleaning costs), lost revenue while the station was unable to operate, and the invoice received from the construction firm.

6. The company recorded $10,000 of supplies as inventory. In previous years, it had written supplies off to expense.

7. ML sold one of its radio stations during the year, at a gain above its cost.

Required:

Assume the role of the auditor of ML. What accounting and reporting treatment would you recommend concerning the above transactions?

A Solution:

1. <u>Objectives</u> of accounting information probably are to facilitate:

   a. Stewardship reporting to public bondholders, in compliance with generally accepted accounting principles, any regulations of securities commissions, any restrictive clauses (covenants) in the Bond Agreement (contract), and other constraints. Public bondholders usually have the right to receive a stewardship report on the status of the company. This report takes the form of audited financial statements. An example of restrictive contract clause (none are hinted at in the case) is that the company must maintain a certain minimum amount of retained earnings. Bondholders have the power to force the company to agree to various terms if the company wishes to borrow. Accountants must be alert to ensure such terms are adhered to; that adequate disclosure exists in the statements, and so on.

   b. Perhaps, in order to postpone income tax payments. This is not nearly as important as objective a.

   The objectives of prediction and evaluation of management by outsiders are not likely to be important unless the bondholders request such information in the general purpose (as opposed to specific purpose) financial statements. Since ML is closely held, its owners would have access to the records of the company or what are called "management accounting" reports.

2. <u>Identification</u> of accounting problems, ranked in order of importance:

   a. Whether or not to capitalize costs incurred during the renovation.

   b. Is a write-down required of the cost of the finished motion picture film carried in inventory?

   c. How to account for the $100,000 owing to Revenue Canada.

   d. How to record and disclose the sale of the radio station.

   e. How to record and disclose the barter transaction.

   f. How to record the option to purchase property.

   g. How to disclose the pending legal suit involving the injured fan.

   h. How to disclose the change in accounting for supplies.

3. <u>Analysis</u> of accounting problems:

Problem a: Some alternative treatments of the renovation costs are:

i. Expense as outlays are incurred (do not capitalize).

ii. Capitalize all of the expenditure by recording the debit to "fixed asset-building." Depreciation at regular rates would ensure such costs are charged to expense over a period of time.

iii. Capitalize some of the expenditures as an asset and amortize the asset over subsequent periods benefited. Only the costs of doing the work once would be capitalized; repairs of work which was previously done incorrectly would be expensed.

Let us consider each type of cost mentioned, looking to facts and objectives. Interest is, for this company, a period cost. It occurs whether the company operates or not. Therefore, the facts suggest i. is most appropriate, unless the interest is incurred during a period of construction when no revenue can be generated.

Labour cost for employees of the radio station did not result in a lasting improvement to the building. An asset exists only when future benefit is forthcoming. Hence, it would not be appropriate to debit such costs to fixed assets. They should be expensed, per i.

Overhead, like interest, is probably a period cost, especially if it is fixed overhead (heat, light, power, and cleaning costs), which occurs regardless of productivity levels. It is very difficult to trace future benefits from fixed overhead expenditures, hence, under the stewardship objective, with emphasis on objectivity, immediate expensing seems more appropriate.

Lost revenue is not a legitimate "cost"; sales will simply be lower for the year. None of the alternatives above directly apply because they refer to costs. But the general concept that an asset must have potential future benefit applies. Lost sales are highly unlikely to produce future benefit.

The invoice received from the construction firm is a legitimate capital or fixed asset, per ii. Presumably, the construction efforts result in an improvement of the building, and future benefits. We match these costs with revenues of later periods.

As a final note, what might the motive be of the controller in his attempted delay of cost recognition? Presumably, he wants to prevent the (perhaps naive) reader of the financial statements from being alarmed by a drop in revenue and extra expenses caused by the accident and the interruption. Perhaps the auditor can convince the controller that there are ways to communicate to readers, through full disclosure. Consider one way:

Note X to Financial Statements:

"The company estimates that it lost revenue of $XX (15/365 of probable annual revenue) while one of its radio stations was closed for renovations for 15 days. In addition, extra labour and related costs of $XX included in wage expense for the year were incurred due to an accident that occurred during the renovation."

Problem b. Some alternative accounting treatments for the motion picture films are:

i. Write the film down to estimated (discounted) present value of cash receipts less cash disbursements expected from distribution of the film.

ii. Leave the carrying cost of the film in inventory as is, and hope for the best. Maybe the critics are wrong?

Looking to the facts, poor reviews by critics are suggestive of, but are probably not sufficiently objective evidence for a loss in value. Under the realization concept, this could justify a write-down, when the objective is stewardship accounting. Students can make other assumptions, but until some experience exists with cash receipts, it is probably too soon for the auditor to press for the write-down. The amount of future cash inflows is still a guess. Hence, ii. makes sense, for now. Notice that we have assumed that revenue is recognized from film sales as they are collected in cash at the box office. If the controller wants to warn bondholders of the financial limitations of the film, a note to the financial statements could explain the situation fully; but a note is not required under stewardship GAAP. Depending on the size of the possible loss (materiality concept), the auditor may insist on such a note disclosure (full disclosure concept). Next year, if cash receipts are low, a write-down can be recorded. Some students may want to record the likely loss this year (conservatism) and may feel that bad reviews from critics are a sufficiently objective indicator. (Observe how the freedom which exists for judgment affects accounting treatment, and why comparability of financial statements among companies is difficult if not impossible to attain.)

Problem c: The $100,000 owing to Revenue Canada appears to represent a prior period adjustment. See Chapter 12 of the text for definitions and the four criteria which must be met in order to qualify as a prior period adjustment. The extra income tax expense relates to 19x7, not to 19x9. Accountants reflect this as an expense of a prior period with the following entry:

Retained earnings $100,000
  Income tax payable $100,000
To record additional income tax expense
for 19x7 as assessed by Revenue Canada.

For the bondholders, what matters is that ML has $100,000 less cash. A complete explanation in a note to the financial statements is called for (full disclosure concept).

Problem d: An assumption is needed because facts are missing. Suppose that the sale of the station was recorded in the accounts properly, maybe with this entry:

Cash	$XXX	
Accumulated depreciation, building	XXX	
Fixed asset, building		$XXX
Gain on sale		XXX

Full disclosure of this item, which is probably an extraordinary transaction under a stewardship objective, might be as follows:

Income Statement

Income before extraordinary item	$XXX
Gain on sale of radio station	
Net of income taxes of $XX (Note 00)	XX

Note 00: "During the year, the company sold one of its radio stations, resulting in a gain net of income taxes of $XXX. Included in 19x9 sales and cost of sales is $XXX and $XXX related to the station which was sold."

Students should note that the disclosure of what the station which was sold contributed to 19x9 sales and cost of goods sold helps bondholders anticipate the change in cash flows next year. Such disclosure does more than accomplish a stewardship objective of the past; it may be helpful for meeting stewardship obligations of the future.

Problem e: Barters or non cash exchanges can be an advanced topic and we will not go into depth on all of the alternative methods of accounting for such transactions. Suffice it to say that ML has revenues (sales of radio advertising time) and expenses (advertising expense) which are not reported on ML's income statement.

Who cares? This is not an easy question to respond to. Income tax officials care, but only when there is an effect on income subject to income tax (called taxable income). The shareholders might care if fair value was not being received for services rendered by the company. Those shareholders who perform ratio analysis might want some form of disclosure, since costs may be incurred to prepare advertising for the newspaper's radio commercial and yet no revenue would appear. (A gross profit ratio may be misleading when compared to previous years.)

If the users care, how should the information be reported: at cost or at retail? Is footnote disclosure adequate or is measurement required?

Some auditors might insist on a journal entry such as:

Advertising expense, at fair value $200,000
   Advertising revenue, at fair value $200,000
To record barter arrangement with newspaper,
at fair value of services rendered by ML.

Presumably, fair value of the ad space in the newspapers is $200,000,
if the space can be sold. If it can be, then this is the sum ML
would settle on instead of receiving cash. If the space cannot be
sold for $200,000, the auditor must struggle with what is fair value
on each side of the transaction.

Problem f: The option to purchase property one year hence has, at
best, a very subjective current market value. If the market price of
the property one year hence is less than $1,000,000, the option (which
gives ML the right to buy the property for $1,000,000) will be worth-
less. ML will lose $10,000. Under the cost concept, the option
would be carried at $10,000 on the 19x9 balance sheet, unless there is
sufficient objective evidence (realization concept) that the market
price of the property one year hence will be less than $1,010,000.
That is, if the price one year hence is likely to be $1,009,000, then
ML will lose $1,000 on the option, since it pays a total of $1,000,000
($10,000 + $1,000,000). In a sense, there is a gain of $9,000, but
the option cost $10,000; a net loss on the option is $1,000. If that
loss is apparent and measurable now (and is material), it should be
accrued in 19x9 per the contingency "rules." Any expected gain should
not be accrued, per conservatism.

A separate issue is what value should be recorded in 19x10, when the
land is purchased. Suppose the market value of the land is $1,020,000
in 19x10. Under the cost concept, the entry will be:

Land $1,010,000
   Option, carried at cost $ 10,000
   Cash   1,000,000
To record purchase of property in 19x10.

Note that the cost of the option is charged to land (cost concept), as
long as the land has a future benefit of $1,010,000.

Problem g: Under the disclosure concept, a note on contingencies would
explain all relevant facts known about the lawsuit at the time the
financial statements are signed. This helps bondholders to predict
the likely impact. If little is known about the lawsuit, little can be
noted in the financial statements. Disclosure aids stewardship of the
future.

Problem h: This could be a minor issue. What dollar amounts are
involved? Is the sum sufficient to affect a user's judgment? Possibly the amount was trivial in the past, but not it may be getting
substantial. Then, a change in accounting policy is warranted. The
auditor draws the reader's attention to changes like this (the
consistency concept) by noting what is called a "consistency qualifi-
cation in the auditor's report. Provided the change is a reasonable

one, bondholders and other readers will probably not object to the change. If the change is made as a result of a change of facts -- such as, the amount is now material -- a retroactive change in accounting principles would not be required.

4. Recommendations:

   a. Expense all costs incurred during the renovation shutdown expect for the costs of the renovation itself, which should be charged to fixed assets. ML may, if it wishes, tell readers what happened (lost revenues, etc.) in a note to the statements. This would meet our stewardship objective of accounting.

   b. It is premature (per the realization concept) to record a write-down on the movie film, but a note of disclosure may be useful to warn readers if potential losses are substantial. Such a note would be useful for a prediction objective, but is not necessary for a stewardship objective, which stresses objectivity.

   c. Record the income tax assessment as a prior period adjustment, since this is required by generally accepted accounting principles (a constraint).

   d. Stewardship objective probably would call for extraordinary treatment of the gain on sale of the radio station. If a prediction objective had been assumed, it would be helpful to disclose the sale of the radio station and its impact on future cash flows (full disclosure concept) in order to help readers predict recurring cash flows.

   e. Stewardship objectives would probably not require disclosure of the barter unless fair value had not been received in the exchange. If prediction, or evaluation of management by outsiders, had been assumed as an objective or purpose of accounting, disclosure would be helpful. The auditor would have to check the facts carefully in order to ensure that fair value had been received.

   f. Accrue for any likely loss (realization concept) in accordance with the contingency rules noted on page 521 of the textbook. The rules are a constraint, in a sense, of stewardship accounting. If a prediction objective had been assumed, additional disclosure would be helpful concerning the option price and the expiry date.

   g. Disclose relevant details about the lawsuit in a contingency note (disclosure concept), if there is anything that can be objectively stated per stewardship objectives. If prediction had been assumed, additional details might be stated, as long as they are not prejudicial to ML's defence.

   h. Draw attention to the change in accounting principles in the auditor's opinion. This is probably a minor issue, however.

13 *Investments in Other Corporations*

Although you may think that every chapter is difficult, this one can be very troublesome unless some fundamental points are always kept in mind:

1. Definitions are important; do not read a section of the textbook or SSP unless you understand the meaning of key terms.

2. It is vital to separate *recording* (meaning journalizing and posting to ledgers) from *reporting* on financial statements. A company can record on one basis but report on another.

3. Do not lose sight of the overall or ultimate purpose of the exercise, which is to provide more informative financial statements for *some,* but not all, users or objectives. (Note, for example, that for income tax purposes, unconsolidated statements are most useful, although other forms might be used if adjusted.)

This chapter is primarily concerned with what are called "intercorporate investments," which means *long term* investments in the *common* voting shares of another company. We are not concerned, in *this* chapter, with short term investments, nor are we discussing investments in other companies in the form of either debt or preferred shares.

RECORDING VERSUS REPORTING

Although there are several ways in which a company might record and also might report its long term investment in the common shares of the another company, we are limiting the discussion in the textbook and SSP to the following:

Alternative Methods of Recording in Ledgers	Alternative Methods of Reporting in Financial Statements
1. Cost method	A. Consolidation
2. Equity method	B. Equity basis
	C. Cost basis

A financial statement for the owner (called an investor) of an intercorporate investment cannot be prepared unless journal entry adjustments (on work sheets, not in the investor's bookds) are made first, to neutralize the recording method used. Different adjustments are needed if the cost method is used instead of the equity method, and vice versa. This adjustment factor must be kept in mind at all times.

Let us illustrate this point. But first, we must review Exhibit 13-1 on page 556 of the textbook. One of the main purposes of the Exbibit is to show that:

1. When the cost method is used, the income of the investor includes any *dividends* received from the company whose common shares were acquired (called the investee). Hence, in order to prepare financial statements of the investor, including therein the financial data of the investee on a consolidation or equity basis, the dividend must be reversed. If it is not reversed, double-counting occurs. That is, both the investor's share of the investee's income plus the dividend paid out of this income would be counted.

2. When the equity method is used, the income of the investor includes the investor's share of the current *income* of the investee. Hence, in order to prepare financial statements of the investor which consolidate the investee or show the investment in it on the cost basis, the income already included in the investor's ledger accounts must be reversed.

If the foregoing is not clear, there is no need to be concerned at this point. The double-counting becomes more noticeable when we discuss work sheets used for preparing consolidated financial statements. Work sheets list the ledger account balances of each company that is to be consolidated. For instance, when the cost method is being used by the investor, its ledger accounts would include the dividend from the investee in the cash account and in the "dividend income" account. If we merely added the revenues and expenses of both the investor and investee without first deleting the "dividend income" amount, we would be counting the investor's share of the investee's income ("dividend income") twice.

SOME TERMINOLOGY

We have already explained the meaning of "intercorporate investment," "investee," and "investor." An investor *reports* the intercorporate investment in its financial statements in accordance with objectives-facts-constraints. For example, a specific user, such as Revenue Canada, may not want consolidated financial statements.

Current constraints, such as the *CICA Handbook*, recommend the following *general* approaches to *reporting*:

1. If over 50% of the voting shares of an investee are owned, the investor would consolidate the accounts of both companies. Consolidation in its simplest sense means to add the balances of the same type of account together, and report the total. That is, rather

than report one figure on the balance sheet for "investment in (investee's name)," we report the total of the investor's and investee's cash, receivables, inventory, and so forth. The reader of the financial statements therefore can obtain a better idea of the consolidated picture, whether the assets are primarily liquid or long term, and so on.

2. If 20% to 50% of the voting shares of an investee are owned, the investor would report the investee on the *equity reporting* basis. This basis is illustrated on pages 581, 52, and 53 of the textbook. The equity basis shows *one figure* for the investment on the balance sheet and one figure on the income statement.

    Both the equity and consolidation bases of reporting must exclude from amounts reported any sums which have not been earned by the consolidated group. A sale of inventory from an investor to an investee at a "profit" cannot be consolidated as a profit unless the investee sells the inventory to outsiders at a "profitable" price. If the investee still holds the purchase from the investor in inventory, the "profit" is considered to be an *unrealized intercompany transaction* and must be eliminated in the consolidation process. Such eliminations occur on work sheets, not in the ledgers of either company.

3. If less than 20% of the voting shares of the investee are held by the investor, the intercorporate investment is called a *portfolio investment*. Such investments are reported at cost on the investor's balance sheets, and the investor's income statement would show only the dividends received from an investee. Unrealized profits on intercompany transactions are *not* eliminated under the cost method. This absence of eliminations helps explain why the cost method is usually not acceptable for reporting intercorporate investments when ownership is in excess of 20%. An investor holding over 20% of the voting shares could manipulate its income too easily by (a) making many artificial sales between an investor and its investees, and (b) declaring or not declaring dividends.

CONSOLIDATED STATEMENTS

The textbook sets our circumstances where consolidated financial statements might be useful and where they are not useful. See pages 548 and 549, for example. Now that you have a general idea of their purpose, it is appropriate to concentrate on the "how-to-do-it." In an introductory course, we do not cover many of the possible situations. However, for those who will not be taking further accounting courses, it is useful to have a list of the more common ones:

1. Investor acquires 100% of the voting common shares of the investee and pays book value (to the shareholders of the investee) for the assets less liabilities (also called net assets, or shareholders' equity).

2. Investor acquires 100% of the voting common shares and pays in excess of book value as recorded on the investee's books:

    (a) If the "excess" payment *exactly* equals the amount by which market value exceeds book value of the investee's net assets, no goodwill arises. On consolidation the investee's net assets tend to be reported at market value on the date of acquisition by the investor.

    (b) If the "excess" payment is *greater* than the amount by which market value exceeds book value of the investee's net assets, good-will arises.

    (c) If the "excess" payment is *less* than the amount by which market value of the investee's net assets exceeds book value, no goodwill arises and special reporting treatment is necessary. This is described in advanced courses.

3. Investor acquires less than 100% of the voting common shares and pays in excess of the book value, per the investee's books, for the percentage of ownership acquired. The same three variations as in 2. arise. In addition, *minority interest* arises; this term is used to indicate the proportion of *book value* of the investee's net assets which were not acquired by the investor.

4. Investor acquires 100% of the voting common shares of the investee and pays less than book value, per the investee's book. In this situation, as with the others, a three way comparison is necessary. For purposes of illustration, arbitrary numbers have been chosen for the book value and market value of the investee's net assets and the purchase price paid by the investor.

    (a) Book value $100 ⎫   On consolidation at the date of
         Market value $ 75 ⎬   acquisition by the investor, market
         Purchase price   ⎪   values of the investee would be used.
           paid by Investor $ 75 ⎭   No goodwill arises.

    (b) Book value $100 ⎫   On consolidation at the date of
         Market value $ 75 ⎬   acquisition by the investor, market
         Purchase price   ⎪   values of the investee would be used.
           paid by Investor $ 80 ⎭   Goodwill of $5 ($80-$75) arises.

    (c) Book value $100 ⎫   This is a special case which is covered
         Market value $ 75 ⎬   in advanced courses. Often, the net
         Purchase price   ⎪   assets would be priced in total at $65
           paid by Investor $ 65 ⎭   on the consolidation at the date of
                                            acquisition.

5. Investor acquires *less than* 100% of the voting common shares of the investee and pays less than book value. Minority interest arises in each of the three situations as noted for 4., and the reporting approach is as described in 4.

Let us now provide some problems to test your understanding of the text-book material and the foregoing points.

NEW PROBLEM 1 (40-70 minutes)

The condensed balance sheets of Investor Ltd. and Investee Ltd. at December 31, 19x5 are as follows:

	Investor Ltd.*	Investee Ltd.
Current assets	$1,000,000	$100,000
Land	200,000	50,000
Building and equipment	1,800,000	800,000
Accumulated depreciation	(500,000)	(200,000)
	$2,500,000	$750,000
Current liabilities	$ 650,000	$100,000
Long term debt payable	800,000	250,000
Common shares	750,000	300,000
Retained earnings	300,000	100,000
	$2,500,000	$750,000

*Prepared prior to the acquisition of Investee Ltd.

Required:

Prepare a consolidated balance sheet at December 31, 19x5 after each of the following unrelated transactions occur as of the close of business on December 31, 19x5:

Case A: Investor buys 100% of the voting shares of Investee Ltd. for $400,000.

Case B: Investor buys 90% of the voting shares of Investee for $360,000.

Case C: Investor buys 100% of the voting shares of Investee for $500,000. The market value of land held by Investee is $150,000.

Case D: Investor buys 100% of the voting shares of Investee for $625,000. Except for land which has a market value of $150,000 all of the other net assets of Investee have a book value which equals market value.

Case E: Same as D except only 50% of the voting common shares are acquired for $625,000.

A Solution:

An assumption is necessary regarding the acquisition of Investee. We have assumed that each acquisition occurs for cash. This means that an entry is necessary on Investor Ltd.'s books:

Investment in Investee Ltd.	$XXX	
Cash (current assets)		$XXX

Consolidation consists of replacing the "investment in Investee Ltd." account with the individual assets and liabilities of Investee Ltd. This can be accomplished by using a work sheet, which is shown in Schedule 13-1. The elimination entry has to reduce the common shares and retained earnings of Investee Ltd. at the date of acquisition to zero by cancelling out the "investment in Investee Ltd." account.

Case A: The entry is:

Common shares of Investee Ltd.	$300,000	
Retained earnings of Investee Ltd.	100,000	
Investment in Investee Ltd.		$400,000

Schedule 13-1

Consolidation Work Sheet

Case A

	Investor Ltd.	Investee Ltd.	Eliminations Debit	Eliminations Credit	Balance Sheet
Current assets	600,000	100,000			700,000
Investment in Investee Ltd.	400,000	–		400,000	
Land	200,000	50,000			250,000
Buildings and equipment	1,800,000	800,000			2,600,000
Accumulated depreciation	(500,000)	(200,000)			(700,000)
	2,500,000	750,000			2,850,000
Current liabilities	650,000	100,000			750,000
Long term debt payable	800,000	250,000			1,050,000
Common shares	750,000	300,000	300,000		750,000
Retained earnings	300,000	100,000	100,000		300,000
	2,500,000	750,000	400,000	400,000	2,850,000

The consolidated balance sheet is prepared from the figures shown in the column at the far right of Schedule 13-1. Observe that the common shares and retained earnings of Investee disappear.

Case B: The work sheet elimination entry is:

Common shares of Investee Ltd.	$300,000	
Retained earnings of Investee Ltd.	100,000	
Investment in Investee Ltd.		$360,000
Minority interest		40,000

The minority interest represents 10% of the common shares plus retained earnings.

- 159 -

Case C: The work sheet elimination entry is:

Common shares	$300,000	
Retained earnings	100,000	
Land	100,000	
Investment in Investee Ltd.		$500,000

The land value has to be increased from $50,000 to $150,000 on the consolidated balance sheet because $150,000 was in effect paid by Investor Ltd. when it bought the voting shares.

Case D: The work sheet elimination entry is:

Common shares	$300,000	
Retained earnings	100,000	
Land	100,000	
Goodwill	125,000	
Investment in Investee Ltd.		$625,000

Goodwill represents the amount paid ($625,000) for the common shares of Investee in excess of the *market value* or fair value of the "identifiable" assets and liabilities acquired. Market value can mean either a buying market or selling market price. (See page 251 of the textbook.) "Identifiable" includes tangible assets and liabilities and some intangible assets; goodwill on the books of Investee Ltd. is not an identifiable asset. Normally a buying market price is used when the investor intends to keep the asset, such as equipment, and use it. A selling market price is used when the asset, such as inventory, is to be sold shortly.

Case E: The work sheet elimination entry is:

Common shares	$300,000	
Retained earnings	100,000	
Land	90,000	
Goodwill	175,000	
Investment in Investee Ltd.		$625,000
Minority interest		40,000

The first tricky part of Case E is that only 90% of the $100,000 excess of market value over book value of Investee's land is recorded. The reason for this is a constraint or current rule of practitioners which holds minority interest at its book value. Investor picks up only its percentage ownership of 90%. In a sense such a practitioners' rule exists because bookkeeping is simplified in complex situations. The remainder of purchase price ($625,000) over market value of assets and liabilities of Investee Ltd. is goodwill.

Consolidation Subsequent to Acquisition Date

Let us follow Case E through to the next year end, December 31, 19x6. During 19x6, Investee operates at a profit, declares a dividend, and buys inventory from Investor, but is not able to sell any of it by December 31, 19x6. Investor made a profit on the inventory sold to Investee.

When consolidating at December 31, 19x6 we must watch for the following:

1. Investor has to amortize the goodwill arising at the date of acquisition. For simplicity we could use a period of 40 years and the straight-line method.

2. What method of *recording* has Investor used for its investment in Investee Ltd.? Cost or equity?

3. The consolidated entity cannot make a profit by selling to itself; hence, any unrealized intercompany profit must be eliminated on the consolidation work sheet.

The trial balances for Investor Ltd. and Investee Ltd. are provided in 13-B.

NEW PROBLEM 2 (60-90 minutes)

The trial balances of Investor Ltd. and Investee Ltd. at December 31, 19x6 are as follows:

	Investor Ltd.		Investee Ltd.	
	Dr.	Cr.	Dr.	Cr.
Current assets	$ 475,000	$	$ 225,000	$
Investment in Investor Ltd.	625,000		–	
Land	200,000		50,000	
Building and equipment	2,000,000		800,000	
Accumulated depreciation		600,000		250,000
Current liabilities		655,000		150,000
Long term debt payable		800,000		250,000
Common shares		750,000		300,000
Retained earnings		300,000		100,000
Sales		1,000,000		650,000
Cost of goods sold	600,000		350,000	
Expenses	250,000		225,000	
Dividends paid	–		50,000	
Dividends received		45,000		
	$4,150,000	$4,150,000	$1,700,000	$1,700,000

Additional information:

Investor sold goods costing it $12,000 to Investee for $18,000. Investee did not sell any of the goods by December 31, 19x6. Investee had not paid Investor for the goods at the year end.

- 161 -

Required:

Prepare consolidated financial statements at December 31, 19x6.

A Solution

By examining the trial balances we can see that Investor used the cost method for recording its investment in Investee Ltd. The elimination entries which would be appropriate are:

a. Common shares $300,000
   Retained earnings   100,000
   Land   90,000
   Goodwill   175,000
     Investment in Investee Ltd. $625,000
     Minority interest   40,000
   This is the entry at the date of acquisition;
   it records the market values and goodwill.

b. Current liabilities $ 18,000
     Current assets $ 18,000
   To eliminate intercompany payable and
   receivable for inventory sale.

c. Dividends received $ 45,000
     Dividends paid $ 45,000
   To eliminate the intercompany dividend.

d. Sales $ 18,000
     Cost of goods sold $ 12,000
     Inventory   6,000
   This entry is easier to understand if we
   show the entries made on each company's
   books at the time of sale:

	Investor's books	Investee's books
i. When inventory originally bought	Inventory $12,000 Cash $12,000	

ii. When
sold
	Due from
	  Investee $18,000
	    Sales $18,000
	
	Cost of
	  goods sold $12,000
	    Inventory $12,000
		Inventory $18,000
		Due to
		  Investor $18,00(

From a consolidation viewpoint no sales took place because you cannot sell to yourself. Since there is no sale, there is no cost of goods sold. There is no profit; hence, inventory on Investee's books must be reduced from $18,000 to $12,000.

- 162 -

e. Expense $ 4,375
        Goodwill $ 4,375
    To amortize one-fortieth of the goodwill
    arising on consolidation.

f. The next entry is tricky; we have to give the minority shareholders
    credit for their 10% ownership in the 19x6 income of $75,000 ($650,000
    less $350,000 less $225,000) of Investee. This means crediting
    minority interest on the balance sheet. The debit is to minority
    interest expense. We have to deduct 10% because we included 100% of
    the sales and expenses of the investee on the work sheet. This entry
    reduces the 100% to 90%:

    Minority interest (income statement) $ 7,500
        Minority interest (balance sheet) $ 7,500

g. We also have to charge 10% of the dividend to minority shareholders
    who received the dividend.

    Minority interest (balance sheet) $ 5,000
        Dividends paid $ 5,000

The consolidated income and retained earnings statements show:

Investor Ltd.

Consolidated Income Statement

Year ended December 31, 19x6

Sales	$1,632,000
Cost of goods sold	938,000
Gross profit	694,000
Expenses	479,375
	$ 214,625
Minority interest	7,500
Net income	$ 207,125

Investor Ltd.

Consolidated Retained Earnings Statement

Year ended December 31, 19x6

Balance, December 31, 19x5	$ 300,000
Add net income	207,125
Balance, December 31, 19x6	$ 507,125

The consolidated balance sheet shows:

Investor Ltd.

Consolidated Balance Sheet

December 31, 19x6

<u>Assets</u>

Current assets		$ 676,000
Land		340,000
Building and equipment	$2,800,000	
Accumulated depreciation	(850,000)	1,950,000
Goodwill		170,625
		$3,136,625

<u>Liabilities</u>

Current liabilities		$ 787,000
Long term debt payable		1,050,000
Minority interest		42,500
Owner's equity:		
Common shares	$750,000	
Retained earnings	507,125	1,257,125
		$3,136,625

If you did not arrive at the same figures as us on your consolidated financial statements, you should prepare a work sheet and post all of our elimination entries. This should help you understand what happened.

EQUITY REPORTING

Equity reporting in its simplest form shows one line on the balance sheet and one on the income statement for the investment and income of the investee. A practice exercise should help.

NEW PROBLEM 3 (20-40 minutes)

Using the same information as for 13-B prepare financial statements for Investor on an equity reporting basis.

A Solution

All effects about Investee Ltd. are put through the two accounts "Investment in Investee Ltd." or "Income from Investee Ltd." and not through "Land," "Goodwill," and so on.

```
Investment account:
  Price paid                                                    $625,000
  90% of income of Investee
        90% x $75,000                                             67,500
                                                                 692,500


  Less:
    Dividends from Investee          $45,000
    Goodwill amortized                 4,375                      49,375
                                                                $643,125


Income account:
  Income less minority interest
        of Investee Ltd.                                        $ 67,500

  Less:
    Goodwill amortized              $ 4,375
    Intercompany unrealized
        profit*                       6,000                      10,375
                                                               $ 57,125
```

*Some accountants include this elsewhere such as in cost of goods sold and sales of Investor Ltd.

Investor Ltd.

Balance Sheet

December 31, 19x6

Assets

```
Current                                                    $   469,000
Investment in Investee Ltd.                                    643,125
Land                                                           200,000
Building and equipment               $2,000,000
  Accumulated depreciation              600,000              1,400,000
                                                            $2,712,125
```

Liabilities

```
Current liabilities                                        $   655,000
Long term debt payable                                         800,000
Owner's equity:
  Common shares                      $  750,000
  Retained earnings                     507,125              1,257,125
                                                            $2,712,125
```

Investor Ltd.

Retained Earnings Statement

Year ended December 31, 19x6

Balance, December 31, 19x5	$ 300,000
Add net income	207,125
Balance, December 31, 19x6	$ 507,125

Investor Ltd.

Income Statement

Year ended December 31, 19x6

Sales	$1,000,000
Cost of goods sold	600,000
Gross profit	400,000
Expenses	250,000
	$ 150,000
Income of Investee Ltd.	57,125
Net income	$ 207,125

If you compare the consolidated statements and those prepared on the equity reporting basis you will note:

1. The word "consolidated" does not appear in the statement titles under the equity reporting basis.

2. The income figures are the same.

3. Under equity basis reporting, except for the "Investment" and "Income of Investee Ltd." accounts, the figures are those of Investor Ltd. The one exception is that we must reduce inventory by the unrealized profit of $6,000.

TEXTBOOK *13-1 (20-30 minutes)

This question requires an assumption before we can respond. If we assume that it is testing our knowledge of constraints, we must look at the CICA Handbook. A suitable response can be found at the beginning of this chapter under "Some Terminology." There are exceptions to the "rules" stated there.

If we ignore constraints, we can look to objectives and facts. Which statement is more informative for: (a) bankers of the investor? (b) bankers of the investee? (c) shareholders of the investor? This was discussed earlier.

14 *Statement of Changes in Financial Position*

The Statement of Changes in Financial Position (SCFP) may be used to provide a variety of perspectives on a company's financial activities besides those shown by the income statement and balance sheet. The main new viewpoints provided by SCFP are:

1. To show changes in "liquidity" -- which may be defined as cash, or working capital, or something else.

2. To show increases and decreases in important long-term asset, liability, and equity accounts -- often called a "disclosure" or "financing and investing" approach.

Some students have difficulty with the SCFP for one or both of the following reasons:

1. They are not sufficiently familiar with the debits and credits of accounting, especially the material in Chapters 3 and 4.

2. They are seeking one way of preparing an SCFP instead of recognizing that different statement designs or formats can be prepared for different purposes.

If you are having trouble with the debits and credits, try to review the material in Chapters 3 and 4 of the textbook and SSP. As far as 2. is concerned, it might be wise to learn the working capital SCFP first. Then, when your confidence has returned, try the others, one at a time.

WORKING CAPITAL (CURRENT ASSETS MINUS CURRENT LIABILITIES)

As noted in the textbook, the working capital type of SCFP *might* be both a liquidity and a disclosure statement, but it often is difficult to accomplish both objectives with one financial statement. However, because its design is closest to the accrual basis of accounting which we have been using in most of the chapter material to date, let us start with working capital.

In a sense there are two focal points for learning about the SCFP:

1. How to compute "funds from operations."

2. How to compute and report other causes of change in funds.

"Funds from operations" refers to the transactions which directly affect the income-earning activities of the business. Rather than treat each of these transactions separately, we group them and call the net effect "funds from operations."

For example, let us review the effect of some income-earning activities on working capital:

A. Sales revenue -- A credit to sales or revenue occurs when we debit cash, accounts receivable or a current liability of unearned revenue. All three debit accounts increase working capital. Hence, they generate or produce "funds from operations."

B. Cost of goods sold -- This account is debited by crediting inventory. When inventory is credited it is reduced, thereby reducing working capital.

C. Selling and administrative expenses, excluding depreciation and amortization -- Selling and administrative expenses are debited when credits are made to cash, accounts payable and prepaid expenses. All three are current or working capital accounts.

D. Depreciation and amortization expense -- The entries setting up debits to depreciation and amortization expense occur by crediting accumulated depreciation or some other non-current account. Such entries lower income but do *not* affect working capital.

The amount of "funds from operations" generated by the following situation as shown by an income statement:

Revenue		$100,000
Cost of goods sold		75,000
Gross profit		25,000
Expenses:		
Selling and administration	$16,000	
Depreciation	6,000	22,000
Income		$ 3,000

We can compute the effect directly (the "forwards" way described in the book) as follows:

	Effect on Working Capital	
	Increases	Decreases
Revenue	$100,000	
Cost of goods sold		$75,000
Selling and administration		16,000
	100,000	91,000
	91,000	
Net increase, or funds generated by operations	$ 9,000	

Because the equation "revenue – expenses = net income" always balances, we can compute funds from operations by adding back to net income those items which lower income but do not affect working capital. In the above example, depreciation lowered income, but did not affect working capital:

Net income	$3,000
Add item which lowered funds but did not increase or decrease a working capital account:	
Depreciation	6,000
Net increase, or funds from operations	$9,000

Let us complicate the computation of funds from operations by adding, separately, two transactions: (1) a gain on sale of a long-lived asset; and (2) income tax expense, some of which is deferred. First, let us consider the gain on sale.

Assume that a depreciable asset costing $50,000 and on which $30,000 of depreciation has accumulated to date, is sold for $26,500. The journal entry on disposal would be:

Cash (a working capital account)	$26,500	
Accumulated depreciation	30,000	
Asset		$50,000
Gain on sale		6,500

This entry may be split into two parts:

(a) Cash	$26,500	
Asset		$26,500

(b) Accumulated depreciation	$30,000	
Asset		$23,500
Gain on sale		6,500

Entry (a) is called a *source* of working capital funds. That is, working capital is increased by a credit to a non-current or non-working capital account.

Entry (b) has two parts -- accumulated depreciation, and the asset -- which are not working capital, and a third -- gain on sale -- which increases net income. The gain therefore has the opposite effect as does depreciation. The sum of $6,500 would have to be *subtracted* from net income to arrive at "funds from operations."

The second complication can be deleted if you did not cover deferred income taxes in your course (Chapter 10). The typical entry when more capital cost allowance (tax depreciation) than depreciation expense has been claimed is:

Income tax expense	$40,000	
Income tax payable		$25,000
Deferred income tax		15,000

The entry may be split into two parts:

(a) Income tax expense	$25,000	
Income tax payable		$25,000

This part, (a), is like cost of goods sold, or selling and administrative expense, and is therefore part of "funds from operations."

The second part of the entry is:

(b) Income tax expense	$15,000	
Deferred income tax		$15,000

The debit is to the income statement and the credit is to a non-current "liability" or "deferred credit." Thus, the effect is the same as for depreciation. Income has been lowered, but working capital has not been increased or decreased.

It is time to test your understanding of funds from operations with a short problem.

NEW PROBLEM 1 (20-40 minutes)

M. Gibbins Ltd. (the company) commenced business on January 1, 19x1. At the end of its first year of operations the financial statements showed:

Current assets		$ 45,000
Long-lived asset, at cost	$100,000	
Less accumulated depreciation	5,000	95,000
		$140,000
Current liabilities		$ 32,500
Deferred income tax		3,500
Owners' equity:		
Common shares	$100,000	
Retained earnings	4,000	104,000
		$140,000

- 170 -

Revenue		$ 80,000
Cost of goods sold		46,600
Gross profit		33,400
Expenses:		
Selling and administration	$20,800	
Gain on sale of asset	(400)	
Depreciation	5,200	25,600
Net income before income tax		7,800
Income tax expense		3,800
Net income		$ 4,000

An examination of the transactions showed:

1. A long-lived asset costing $10,000, on which $200 of depreciation had accumulated, was sold for $10,200.
2. Of the income tax expense of $3,800, only $300 was payable in cash or due within the next year.
3. Long-lived assets of $110,000 were purchased for cash.

Required:

a. Compute funds from operations for 19x1.
b. If you need the practice, try preparing a working capital SCFP for 19x1.

A Solution

a. If we use the "forward" or direct way of computing funds from operations the following are considered:

Revenue	$+80,000
Cost of goods sold	−46,600
Selling and administrative expense	−20,800
Income tax payable	− 300
	$ 12,300

Using the "backwards" way:

Net income		$ 4,000
Add:		
Depreciation	$ 5,200	
Income tax deferred	3,500	8,700
		12,700
Deduct gain on sale		400
		$ 12,300

b. When we use the working capital SCFP it is useful to first compute what we are trying to balance to:

Working capital at end of year:
   (Current assets less current liabilities)
      $45,500 − $32,500 $12,500

Working capital at beginning of year is
   zero because the company is new   0

Increase in working capital in 19x1 $12,500

Which transactions increased working capital?   Three did:

1. Funds from operations
2. Sale of common shares
3. Proceeds on sale of long-lived assets

How do we know only the three did, assuming that operations can be
regarded as one? We reconstructed the journal entries, as described
in the textbook. For example, the sale of shares entry is:

    Cash (a working capital account) $100,000
       Common shares $100,000

Also, the entry on disposal of the long-lived assets is:

    Cash $ 10,200
    Accumulated depreciation   200
       Long-lived asset $ 10,000
       Gain on sale of asset   400

If we split this entry into its two parts, we can see that working
capital has been increased by $10,200 (and not some other figure such
as $10,000 or $9,800).

Which transactions decreased working capital? Only one did, the purchase of long-lived assets for $110,000.

Our SCFP therefore is:

                          M. Gibbins Ltd.

             Statement of Changes in Financial Position

                    Year ended December 31, 19x1

Sources of working capital:
   Funds from operations (generally the details
      would be provided) $ 12,300
   Proceeds on sale of long-lived asset   10,200
   Sale of common shares   100,000
                                                                  122,500

Use of working capital:
   Acquisition of long-lived assets   110,000
Increase in working capital $ 12,500

What does the SCFP tell us? Overall it conveys two important matters:

1. The company financed its long-lived assets by issuing long term equity.
2. The funds from operations helped to increase working capital. Point 1. is important for liquidity. If we finance our long-lived assets with short-term debt, we could easily go bankrupt. That is, the debtor could ask for repayment, but there would be no liquid assets available for repayment.

In addition, the SCFP tells us that although the net figure for "long-lived asset, at cost" on the December 31, 19x1 balance sheet is $100,000, this was the result of two transactions during the year. One was the $110,000 purchase, and the other was disposal proceeds of $10,200 (not $10,000). Knowing about these two transactions may not seem important for a small company such as Gibbins. However, knowing both increases and decreases could be very important to some readers. For example, a company may not have any bank loan at the beginning or the end of a year. From a review of comparative balance sheets, it may appear to be too conservatively managed and not be getting the benefits of lower cost debt. But, the SCFP may show that it borrowed $1,000,000 from a bank, and repaid this sum before year end. In short, the company had sufficient borrowing power to be granted a $1,000,000 loan, and also had enough cash to later repay the loan. Such SCFP information indicates a strength about the company that would otherwise be unknown by viewing balance sheets and income statements.

TEXTBOOK *14-4: A SOLUTION (15-25 minutes)

This question is a little harder than you might suspect. Pages 616 and 617 of the textbook give several clues. But, the question can be answered in greater depth.

There are probably two main reasons why a working capital statement design is widely used in Canada:

1. Unfortunately, many preparers do not seem to be aware of the alternative designs, and tend to follow an approach that they were taught many years ago. (Users must therefore be on guard for uninformative SCFP.)

2. Working capital is close to accrual accounting in the sense that many accruals affect working capital accounts. It is therefore: (a) easier to compute "funds from operations," and (b) possible to highlight the less frequent transactions such as acquisitions of long-lived assets and changes in debt and equity.

If we view the SCFP as a statement of disclosure, reason 2.(b) has considerable merit. That is, by reporting transactions which have longer term effects, information is available to those who want to evaluate management and attempt to predict.

Managers of smaller companies would have to keep track of their cash
flows so that they could invest excess cash for short periods, or borrow
when necessary. A cash definition of funds would be helpful to them.
For example, in the early 1980's, interest rates on bank accounts soared
in Canada. This meant that many small businesses had to find extra cash
in order to meet interest payments. Such extra cash would have to come
from operations. If interest payments could not be met, bankruptcy could
result.

Larger businesses have a continuous flow in and out of such accounts as
cash, receivables, payables, inventory, and so forth. Since these accounts
are working capital items, together they *may* be a good gauge of liquidity
(or the ability to repay current liabilities) movements or *trends*. The
trends are worth watching, if we want to avoid a liquidity crisis and
potential bankruptcy. Hence, in the short term (one month), working
capital may not be a good measure of liquidity but in the intermediate
term (say six months), working capital trends could be worth watching.

There is some evidence that firms approaching bankruptcy tend to sell
their long-lived assets, thereby increasing working capital. Therefore
users should be on guard against such firms' artificially increasing their
working capital rather than presenting genuine increases that arise from
operations or permanent financing.

The theme of the chapter is that the SCFP should be tailored to fit the
situation: the type of company, its objectives, the facts, etc. Sometimes preparers may not be willing to cater to the needs of users because
of cost or legal liability considerations, but these tend to be of less
significance for the SCFP.

ALTERNATE DESIGNS

The material in this section may be more advanced than your instructor
wishes to cover, and therefore might be passed over. Those who wish to
take additional accounting courses should find it useful.

In designing an SCFP we must be concerned about *two* decisions:

1. The definition of "funds."
2. The definition and computation of "funds from operations."

The two decisions are separable. For example, "funds from operations"
could be computed as described in New Problem 1, which is a combination
of accrual accounting and working capital, whereas funds might be
"cash." New Problem 2 illustrates the different designs in a simple
situation.

NEW PROBLEM 2 *(20-40 minutes)*

D. McDonald Ltd. commenced business on January 1, 19x2 with $5,000 cash.
During the year, the company provided consulting services for $12,500,
but did not incur any costs. At December 31, 19x2, the $12,500 was

still not received; it was received in cash in late January 19x3. The
balance sheet of the company was as follows at December 31, 19x2:

Cash	$ 5,000	Capital	$ 5,000
Accounts receivable	12,500	Retained earnings	12,500
	$17,500		$17,500

Required:

Prepare an SCFP on each of the following bases:

	Definition of Funds	Definition of Funds From Operations
a.	Working Capital	Accrual – working capital
b.	Cash	Accrual – working capital
c.	Cash	Cash

A Solution

a. Working capital increased from zero to $17,500 during 19x2. The
income statement would show revenue of $12,500, no expenses and an
income of $12,500. Funds from operations therefore would be $12,500.
The SCFP therefore is:

D. McDonald Ltd.

Statement of Changes in Financial Position

Year ended December 31, 19x2

Sources of working capital:	
From operations	$12,500
Investment by owner	5,000
Increase in working capital	$17,500

b. Cash has increased by $5,000 but funds from operations is $12,500.
The SCFP could show either:

i.   D. McDonald Ltd.

Statement of Changes in Financial Position

Year ended December 31, 19x2

Sources of cash:	
Investment by owner	$ 5,000
Uses of cash:	
Nil	0
Increase in cash	$ 5,000

or, ii.   D. McDonald Ltd.

Statement of Changes in Financial Position

Year ended December 31, 19x2

Sources:
  From operations $12,500
  Investment by owner   5,000
                                              $17,500

Uses:
  Investment in accounts receivable   12,500
  Increase in cash $ 5,000

Method ii. shows funds from operations, even though cash is not directly involved.

c. Funds from operations on a cash basis is nil, but cash increased by $5,000. The SCFP would show:

D. McDonald Ltd.

Statement of Changes in Financial Position

Year ended December 31, 19x2

Sources of cash:
  From operations:
    Net income $12,500
    Less revenue on account which increased
      income but did not increase cash   12,500
                                         0

  Investment by owner   5,000
  Increase in working capital $ 5,000

If you work with the three (or four) SCFP above until you understand different effects, you are well on your way to understanding SCFP fully. They are designed to communicate information, and each fits a different set of circumstances. Try designing a problem of your own and answering it using a variety of SCFP formats.

FINANCING AND INVESTING

We will conclude this chapter with a problem that provides a set of facts which lend themselves more to a financing and investing format than to working capital or cash. Before attempting Problem 3, it would be wise to review pages 631 to 640 of the textbook.

NEW PROBLEM 3 (40-80 minutes)

T. Var Ltd. was incorporated on January 1, 19x3 with an investment of $100,000. During 19x3, the following transactions occurred:

1. Building and equipment costing $200,000 was acquired by paying $20,000 cash and signing a mortgage for the balance. By December 31, 19x3, principal of $7,000 and interest of $23,000 had been paid on the mortgage.

2. Inventory of $75,000 was acquired on account. By December 31, 19x3 $61,500 of the liability had been paid in cash.

3. Inventory costing $68,300 was sold on account for $129,000. By December 31, 19x3, $90,000 of the accounts receivable were collected in cash.

4. Selling and administrative expenses, excluding depreciation and interest, amounted to $18,240. Depreciation expense of $5,000 was charged.

5. A dividend of $2,000 was declared, but not paid.

6. The mortgage holder agreed to accept common shares of $100,000 in exchange for $100,000 of principal on the mortgage.

7. Equipment costing $10,000, on which depreciation of $500 had accumulated, was sold at a loss of $375.

8. Income tax of $6,000 was paid in cash; no deferrals existed.

Required:

a. Prepare a balance sheet at December 31, 19x3 and an income statement for 19x3.

b. Prepare an appropriate SCFP for 19x3.

Solution

a.

T. Var Ltd.

Balance Sheet

December 31, 19x3

Assets		Liabilities and Owners' Equity	
Current assets:		Current liabilities:	
Cash	$ 63,385	Accounts payable	$ 13,500
Accounts receivable	39,000	Dividend payable	2,000
Inventory	6,700		15,500
	109,085	Mortgage payable	73,000
Building and equipment	190,000	Owners' equity:	
Less accumulated		Common shares	200,000
depreciation	4,500	Retained earnings	6,085
	185,500		206,085
	$294,585		$294,585

- 177 -

T. Var Ltd.

Income Statement

Year ended December 31, 19x3

Revenue		$129,000
Cost of goods sold		68,300
Gross profit		60,700
Expenses:		
Selling and administration	$18,240	
Interest	23,000	
Depreciation	5,000	
Loss on disposal of equipment	375	46,615
		14,085
Income taxes		6,000
Net income		$ 8,085

T. Var Ltd.

Statement of Retained Earnings

Year ended December 31, 19x3

Net income for the year	$ 8,085
Deduct dividends	2,000
Balance, December 31, 19x3	$ 6,085

b. If we use the T-account method of preparing an SCFP, "funds from operations" would be computed by the "backwards" method. Appropriate journal entries for a working capital format are:

   i. Funds from operations $ 8,085
           Retained earnings $ 8,085

   This represents the closing entry.

  ii. Building and equipment $200,000
        Cash (working capital) $ 20,000
        Mortgage payable   180,000

 iii. Mortgage payable $ 7,000
        Cash (working capital) $ 7,000

    Note: No entry would be made for interest expense because it is part of funds from operations included under i. above with the backwards method. Entries are not needed for other revenue and expense items which are offset to *working capital* accounts.

| iv. | Funds from operations | $ 5,000 | |
| | Accumulated depreciation | | $ 5,000 |

| v. | Retained earnings | $ 2,000 | |
| | Dividend payable (working capital) | | $ 2,000 |

| vi. | Mortgage payable | $100,000 | |
| | Common shares | | $100,000 |

vii.	Cash (working capital)	$100,000	
	Common shares		$100,000
	Initial issue on incorporation of company.		

ix.	Cash (working capital)	$ 9,125	
	Accumulated depreciation	500	
	Loss on sale (funds from operations)	375	
	Equipment		$ 10,000

Next, we should post the above journal entries to the special T-accounts and note any items which would help us prepare a financing and investing format of SCFP. The change in working capital is $93,585 ($109,085 less $15,500).

Working capital				Retained earnings				Building and equipment			
	93,585						6,085	190,000			
(vii)	100,000	(ii)	20,000	(v)	2,000	(i)	8,085	(ii) 200,000		(ix)	10,000
(ix)	9,125	(iii)	7,000								
(x)	13,460	(v)	2,000								

Mortgage payable				Accumulated depreciation				Common shares			
			73,000				4,500				200,000
		(ii)	180,000	(ix)	500	(iv)	5,000			(vi)	100,000
(iii)	7,000									(vii)	100,000
(vi)	100,000										

Funds from operations			
(i)	8,085		
(iv)	5,000		
(ix)	375		
	13,460		
		(x)	13,460

- 179 -

Another journal entry is needed to close "funds from operations" to working capital to check that the latter balances.

x.   Working capital $13,460
         Funds from operations $13,460

The SCFP can now be prepared *primarily* by looking at two T-accounts: funds from operations, and working capital. We say "primarily" because it helps to remember three types of transactions for the financing and investing SCFP:

1.   Barters or non-cash exchanges between noncurrent accounts.
2.   Conversions or switches between long-term liability and owners' equity accounts.
3.   Major changes in individual working capital accounts.

The existence of one or more of these three transactions could signify that a financing format would communicate better than a working capital design.

One possible SCFP, based on working capital changes, would appear as follows:

T. Var Ltd.

Statement of Changes in Financial Position

Year ended December 31, 19x3

Sources:
   Funds from operations $ 13,460
   Investment by owner   100,000
   Proceeds on sale of equipment   9,125
                                                                    122,575

Uses:
   Purchase of buildings and equipment $20,000
   Repayment of principal on mortgage   7,000
   Dividend declared   2,000   29,000

Increase in working capital $ 93,585

If we felt that the foregoing design was not adequate disclosure for a particular user group we could recast the information.

T. Var Ltd.

Statement of Changes in Financial Position

Year ended December 31, 19x3

Financing transactions:		
Funds from operations		$ 13,460
Less dividends		2,000
Available for investing		11,460
Investment by owners		100,000
		$111,460
Investing transactions:		
Purchase of building and equipment		$200,000
Less:		
Mortgage less payments of $7,000	$ 73,000	
Mortgage converted to common shares	100,000	
Proceeds of sale of some equipment	9,125	182,125
		17,875
Increase in working capital excluding cash		30,200
Cash		63,385
		$111,460

This type of SCFP focuses on transactions instead of liquidity. Note
that considerably more information is provided than the straightforward
working-capital SCFP. Is such information useful? It depends on the
users' needs. We cannot give one, all-purpose answer.

15 *Financial Statements: The Perspective of the Analyst*

OVERVIEW

Chapter 15 in the textbook indicates that there are many types of analysts. Some are: trust company loan officers; bankers; stock brokers; insurance company researchers looking for securities in which to invest insurance premiums; finance company analysts; venture capital company analysts; investigators for conglomerate companies desiring to diversify; and so forth. They may look at quite a range of companies. In addition, some may be clerks who like to calculate ratios, even those which are meaningless; others could conduct sophisticated analysis.

In view of this diversity, it is difficult to summarize analytical approaches in just one chapter. For instance, an analyst for a brokerage house may want to assemble a portfolio of a dozen or so investments for a client. In such situations the analyst would focus, among other matters, on *risk* of loss of the funds. She would not want to put "all of the investor's eggs into one basket." Stocks with offsetting risk potential would be sought. Such accounting and disclosure as diversified or segment reporting (pages 534 and 535 of the textbook) would be especially important.

In contrast, a banker wishing to make a loan to a small business might be able to learn much from ratio analysis of current operations. Gross profit and expense trends over recent years could help to spot weaknesses in the company. Some of the other ratios on pages 680 to 682 might also prove helpful when the financial statements are relatively free of accounting "gimmickry." This could occur, for example, when the financial statements are *not* prepared solely to minimize income tax.

Analysts have to be aware of the thinking and constraints of the preparer of the financial statements. Sometimes analysts have to guess about the environment of the preparer; on other occasions, analysts may be able to talk directly to preparers. Trends in GAAP, such as are occurring with liabilities (see chapter 10 in this book), have to be known by analysts. The material on pages 660 and 661 ought to be understood. In total, all we can say is that some analysts know what they are doing; others may use poor sources of information and narrow thinking. Analysis is very much an "art" using considerable judgment.

TEXTBOOK *15-1: A SOLUTION (15-25 minutes)

Preparers and users of financial statements could easily have different
objectives or purposes in mind. As a result, information prepared for one
purpose may not be suitable for a specific need of a user of financial
statements. For example, the preparer of information may view stewardship
as the major accounting objective because of the legal constraints of
Company and Securities acts. As a result, historic cost financial statements in accordance with GAAP would be prepared. A user concerned with
determining the value of this company would need to understand the purpose
for which the financial statements were prepared, recognize the limitations
of the historic costs statements, and seek additional information on the
company's cash generating ability and net realizable value of its net
assets. Failure to recognize the need for a different type of financial
information for the specific decision of determining the company's value,
say for arriving at a purchase price for a company, could lead to a poor
decision.

Similarly, analysts interpreting the financial results of a company must
understand the accounting alternatives that exist, identify the alternative selected by the company, evaluate whether the method selected is
appropriate for assessing the company's potential, and make adjustments
where necessary. For example, a construction company may use the completed contract method of recognizing construction revenue for income
tax purposes (i.e., to defer taxes). An analyst, in evaluating the cash
generating ability of the company would need to recognize the purpose of
the statements and make adjustments to reflect the profit to be earned
on the project in progress and the amount and timing of cash inflows
and outflows.

NEW PROBLEM 1 (30-90 minutes)

Assume that you are a financial analyst employed by a stock broker.
Your employer has received a request from a client who is considering
the acquisition of a 55% common share interest in either A Ltd. or B Ltd.
The client intends to investigate the two companies, which are in the
same line of business, in considerable detail, before making an offer to
the present owners. However, the client wants a preliminary analysis of
each of the two companies based on their financial statements. She would
like a report listing of matters which should be investigated further in
each company in order to ascertain whether a problem exists. This listing is to be based on your review of the financial statements. She would
also like your recommendation, with reasons, concerning which company of
the two seems to be the better, assuming a 55% ownership of each would
cost roughly the same amount.

Condensed, unaudited financial statements are the only ones available
at this point. You may assume that the present date is early 19x4.

Income Statements:

	A Ltd. (in thousands of dollars)			B Ltd. (in thousands of dollars)		
	19x3	19x2	19x1	19x3	19x2	19x1
Revenue	$6,000	$ 5,500	$5,000	$6,000	$5,500	$5,000
Cost of goods sold	3,100	2,700	2,350	2,950	2,450	2,100
Gross profit	2,900	2,800	2,650	3,050	3,050	2,900
Expenses	1,100	1,050	1,000	850	800	750
Income before income tax	1,800	1,750	1,650	2,200	2,250	2,150
Income tax	900	875	825	1,000	1,000	1,050
Net income	$ 900	$ 875	$ 825	$1,200	$1,150	$1,100

Balance Sheets:

	A Ltd. (in thousands of dollars)			B Ltd. (in thousands of dollars)		
	19x3	19x2	19x1	19x3	19x2	19x1
Cash	$ 100	$ 200	$ 500	$ 100	$ 200	$ 500
Receivables	1,000	800	800	1,100	900	900
Inventory	1,400	850	850	1,150	700	600
	2,500	1,850	2,150	2,350	1,800	2,000
Assets held under lease	275	300	325	–	–	–
Plant and equipment	10,725	10,500	9,275	11,150	10,950	9,910
	11,000	10,800	9,600			
Accumulated depreciation	3,000	2,700	2,400	3,000	2,850	2,710
	8,000	8,100	7,200	8,150	8,100	7,200
	$10,500	$ 9,950	$9,350	$10,500	$9,900	$9,200
Accounts payable and accrued liabilities	$ 1,400	$ 1,350	$1,050	$ 1,900	$1,600	$1,200
Income tax payable	150	125	100	100	100	100
	1,550	1,475	1,150	2,000	1,700	1,300
Deferred income tax	200	80	10			
Long term debt	1,000	1,000	1,000			
Present value of lease obligation	250	270	290			
Owners' equity:						
Capital	5,000	5,000	5,000	6,000	6,000	6,000
Retained earnings	2,500	2,125	1,900	2,500	2,200	1,900
	7,500	7,125	6,900	8,500	8,200	7,900
	$10,500	$ 9,950	$9,350	$10,500	$9,900	$9,200

Retained Earnings
    Statements:

	A Ltd. (in thousands of dollars)			B Ltd. (in thousands of dollars)		
	19x3	19x2	19x1	19x3	19x2	19x1
Balance, January 1	$2,125	$1,900	$3,475	$2,200	$1,900	$1,650
Net income	900	875	825	1,200	1,150	1,050
	3,025	2,775	2,650	3,400	3,050	2,700
Dividends	525	650	750	900	850	800
Balance, December 31	$2,500	$2,125	$1,900	$2,500	$2,200	$1,900

Required:

Prepare the report requested by the client.

A Solution

You will have noticed that we gave a wide time range for this problem or case. By making assumptions, you can make the learning experience broad or narrow. For further comments in this regard, see pages 237-247 of the textbook. You have freedom in the case to show what you have learned in this course, or to dismiss the exercise as not relevant to the client's decision process.

You have been asked for two analyses: (1) matters that arise from a review of the financial statements and that appear to need further investigation; (2) a supported recommendation of either A Ltd. or B Ltd.

Let us start with the proposition that the two companies are *identical* in their business practices and prospects for the immediate future, and that the financial statement differences are caused strictly by accounting principles and practices. If we *cannot* prove that they are identical, then we have some basis for recommending one over the other.

Net Income Differences: These could be caused by different accounting for identical transactions:

1. A uses income tax allocation whereas B does not. This causes A's income to be lower.

2. A may use LIFO in a period of rising prices and B may use FIFO. B's income would thus be higher.

3. A may expense expenditures which are not clearly betterments or repairs, but a mixture of both; B may capitalize them, thereby expensing them through depreciation over a longer time frame.

4. A must expense interest on the long term debt, but B has $1,000,000 in equity. B also has higher dividends but these are not income statement charges.

5. Both companies may be leasing some assets and only A is capitalizing the leases. The effect of this on net income is not clear to us; interest expense plus depreciation under capitalization could be more or less than the lease payments. See pages 448 to 450 of the textbook.

6. B appears to be depreciating its assets over a longer period of time. The difference in accumulated depreciation in A between 19x2 and 19x3 is double that of B.

Valuation and Liquidity Differences:

1. The two companies have identical cash balances but A has the stronger working capital position. This arises because A has higher inventory and lower accounts payable and accrued liabilities. *If* we accept the previous comment that A's lower income is caused by its use of LIFO, then how do we explain that A's inventory is *higher* than B's? Since B's gross profit percentage (gross profit to revenue) is higher than A's we might indeed conclude that it uses FIFO. Or, we might conclude that it is able to buy inventory at lower prices. We definitely have to look into what is causing the differences in cost of goods sold and inventory. The financial statements alone are not conclusive. Perhaps A has too much costly inventory on hand. This would increase storage costs and may also be risking obsolescence charges.

   In the past two years B's working capital position has worsened because of increasing accounts payable and decreasing cash. Both of these should be investigated.

2. If B is going to borrow from the general public it may have to comply with GAAP. Thus, it may have to capitalize its leases which are in substance purchases. Also it may have to employ tax allocation and record deferred income tax.

3. We must investigate why A has issued $1,000,000 of debt and B has common share capital $1,000,000 higher than A. When does A's debt come due? If soon, we may have a financing and liquidity problem.

   The leverage aspects of A's $1,000,000 debt must be considered. This subject is discussed on pages 494-496 of the textbook. Maybe B is too conservatively financed.

4. The depreciation and capitalization policy of both companies merits further study. Are identical assets being accounted for one way in A and another in B? See pages 390-392 of the textbook.

5. Dividend policy is worth checking. Somehow in the past two years, B has paid more dividends per dollar of capital than A. Where did the cash come from? Is this why the accounts payable of B have increased? Is B risking trouble from creditors, or are the payables not a problem?

<u>Overall</u>: Our financial statement analysis has raised some interesting issues. Without footnotes and similar explanations within the body of the financial statements we have to guess, or defer judgment. We really cannot say that one is a better investment than the other. The review of analysts' reports in Chapter 15 indicates the type of factors they consider, and we know little about these.

Although we may think that differences in the financial statements have been caused by *more* than accounting policy alternatives, we are not sure of ourselves. One of the benefits of statement analysis is that it has pinpointed some areas requiring further study. Without this further study we would be foolish to recommend one company over the other.

Your response may have been more comprehensive than ours, especially if you calculated many ratios. As long as you explained the significance of the ratios which you computed, and avoided crunching meaningless ratios, you probably gave a good response.

16 *General Price Level Restatements and Current Value Accounting*

Some of the main themes of Chapter 16 and of portions of other chapters are:

1. Each of the measurement systems (historic cost; general price level restatement of historic cost; and current value or current cost) can be sensibly applied or can fit a specific set of objectives-facts-constraints. In an introductory course, it is not possible to explain the exact set which fits each measurement. But we can work towards this goal by not letting ourselves think that there is one all-purpose measurement system. When we carefully list costs and benefits, we can say that each has its place. For example, under current income tax law in Canada, it is best to start with historic cost and then make modifications to satisfy income tax law.

2. In order to determine a *lifetime* (i.e., from commencement to the windup of a business) income, it is necessary to choose a definition of capital maintenance. For instance, "capital" (owners' equity sometimes excluding retained earnings) may be maintained in original investment (or money historic capital) terms, meaning the amount of dollars originally invested in the business. When we choose such a definition we have ignored the fact that the purchasing power of a dollar changes over time. Our focus therefore is the dollar, and *not* what the dollar will buy in goods and services.

   People invest, or start up a business, rather than consume or spend the money put into the business because they hope to *make a return on their investment*. (See Chapter 6.) Presumably a return on investment allows them to be able to consume more at a later date than they otherwise could have by not having invested. Thus, focussing on a dollar, rather than on what the dollar will buy, does not appear sensible for investors. Since many investors want to evaluate management and predict cash flows, "money historic capital" maintenance has serious limitations for them.

3. Disclosure plays an important role in financial reporting. In some circumstances it is possible that note disclosure of key figures, such as cost of goods sold at current cost, in a historic cost financial statement, may satisfy many users. Two complete sets of financial statements, one based on historic and the other on replacement cost, may be too costly to prepare, given the benefits.

4. At least two pieces of information must be compared before an assessment can be made. Considerable personal discipline is necessary to ensure that we pause before making a judgment and clearly *identify* what we are comparing to what. (This point is illustrated as well on pages 252 and 253 of the textbook.) We cannot choose measurements wisely unless we know what judgments we want to make.

5. Accounting measurements generally are not neutral in their effect on the judgment or attitude of people. It is possible to manipulate some people by measuring their performance one way instead of another. Other people may be able to "see through" the measurements and the impact they are having. We have to be careful not to generalize the results or effects of changing from one type of measurement to some other.

6. A traditional historic cost reporting system or package of financial statements contains more than one measurement. For example, accounts receivable are usually shown at net realizable value. Inventory might be reported at replacement cost when this is less than original cost. Some receivables and payables might be priced on a discounted present value basis. We must be on guard to look for combinations of measurements that may serve a user's needs, and to try not to wed our thinking to one measurement basis.

GENERAL PRICE LEVEL RESTATEMENTS

General price level restatements can be made to more than historic cost figures and systems. For example, we could general price level restate replacement costs using a general price index. In an introductory textbook, we have restricted our restatements to historic cost (GPL).

During the 1970's, accountants in several countries experimented with supplementary GPL financial statements because inflation rates were quite high. By the 1980's, accounting bodies had become lukewarm about the benefits of supplementary GPL for users' needs. The main group of critics of historic cost simply were not overjoyed with supplementary financial statements that are tied so closely to historic cost. Little *new* information is provided by GPL's of historic cost. As page 729 of the textbook indicates, some people confuse GPL with a current value measurement.

Practice in doing a GPL restatement of historic cost will help in understanding the strengths and limitations of the reports for different users. One of the keys to understanding GPL is to be able to ascertain whether an account is monetary or nonmonetary. The question to ask yourself is: will the price be capable of rising in a period of inflation? Canadian dollars (cash) are fixed in amount, and will not rise; they are therefore "monetary." Accounts receivable are "monetary" as long as a fixed sum of dollars will be paid. In a few countries with high inflation, payment may be required in general purchasing power equivalents and not in dollars; such receivables would be nonmonetary. Inventory, which has already been sold at a definite price, and will be delivered in the future, is a monetary asset. Inventory which has not been sold is free to rise in dollars of "worth" during inflation; it is therefore nonmonetary. This type of thinking can be extended to other assets and liabilities. Monetary assets and liabilities do not require restatement, whereas nonmonetary items do.

NEW PROBLEM 1 (50-80 minutes)

B. Irvine Ltd. commenced business on January 1, 19x1, with $5,000,000, which was credited to common share capital. On January 1, 19x2, the company bought $10,000,000 of plant and equipment which it still owns. The financial statements for the year ended December 31, 19x5 show:

B. Irvine Ltd.

Income Statement

Year ended December 31, 19x5

Revenue		$8,000,000
Expenses:		
Depreciation	$1,000,000	
Other	5,000,000	6,000,000
Income		$2,000,000

B. Irvine Ltd.

Balance Sheets

Years ended December 31

	19x5	19x4
Assets		
Monetary assets	$ 5,300,000	$ 2,000,000
Plant and equipment	$10,000,000	$10,000,000
Accumulated depreciation	4,000,000	3,000,000
	6,000,000	7,000,000
	$11,300,000	$ 9,000,000

Liabilities

Monetary liabilities	$ 1,500,000	$ 1,200,000
Owners' equity:		
Capital	5,000,000	5,000,000
Retained earnings	4,800,000	2,800,000
	9,800,000	7,800,000
	$11,300,000	$ 9,000,000

The general price index over the first five years showed:

January 1, 19x1	40.0
January 1, 19x2	50.0
January 1, 19x5	100.0
Average for 19x5	112.5
December 31, 19x5	125.0

For simplicity it may be assumed that "other expenses" and "revenue" were paid or received in cash or monetary items.

Required:

Case A: In this situation, assume that "other expenses" and "revenue" were paid and received just before the close of business on December 31, 19x5.

Case B: In this situation, assume that "other expenses" and "revenue" were paid and received at mid year 19x5 when the general price index was 112.5.

For each of Case A and Case B, prepare general price level restated historic cost balance sheets at December 31, 19x5 and December 31, 19x4, and an income statement for 19x5 in dollars of general purchasing power as of December 31, 19x5. (The latter requirement means to use general price index number 125 in the numerator of the fraction needed for restatements.)

A Solution

Let us do Case A first. Then if you have trouble with Case A, you can try to do Case B again before reading the solution to B. We have used Problem 1 many times with classes, and have found that a large number of students have difficulty with the income statement portion of it. You may want to check your answer before reading any further in these notes.

Case A

The easiest place to start is with the December 31, 19x5 balance sheet, because the monetary items are already in dollars of *general* purchasing power at December 31, 19x5. Only the nonmonetary items need be adjusted from the date of purchase to dollars of general purchasing power at December 31, 19x5.

Balance sheet at December 31, 19x5:

Monetary assets: $5,300,000 x $\frac{125}{125}$ $ 5,300,000

Plant and equipment: $10,000,000 x $\frac{125}{50}$

  (The plant was bought when the general
   price index was 50)   25,000,000

Accumulated depreciation: $4,000,000 x $\frac{125}{50}$

  (The depreciation is based on the original cost
  of the asset, when the general index was 50,
  and not on the index when the cost allocation
  or depreciation journal entry was made.)   (10,000,000)

                                                $20,300,000

Monetary liabilities: $1,500,000 x $\frac{125}{125}$ 1,500,000

Owners' equity:
  Capital: $5,000,000 x $\frac{125}{40}$ 15,625,000

  Retained earnings:
   (This is the balancing figure. We could
   prove it if we had data on transactions
   from January 1, 19x1 to date.)   3,175,000

                                                $20,300,000

Balance sheet at December 31, 19x4:

In order to restate this balance sheet to dollars of general purchasing power at December 31, 19x5, we have to:

1. Restate the *non*-monetary items to dollars of general purchasing power at December 31, 19x4.

2. Roll forward the restated balance sheet items to dollars of general purchasing power at December 31, 19x5. This means multiplying everything on the balance sheet by 125/100. We then have compara- tive years' balance sheets (at December 31, 19x4 and 19x5) both stated in dollars of general purchasing power at December 31, 19x5.

The comparative balance sheets, both stated in dollars of general purchas- ing power at December 31, 19x5, can then be used to check on the accuracy of your restated income statement. Have you balanced income to the change in restated retained earnings?

Restated to dollars of general purchasing power at December 31, 19x4:

Monetary assets: $2,000,000 x $\frac{100}{100}$ $ 2,000,000

Plant and equipment: $10,000,000 x $\frac{100}{50}$ 20,000,000

Accumulated depreciation: $3,000,000 x $\frac{100}{50}$ (6,000,000)

                                                                                                          $16,000,000

Monetary liabilities: $1,200,000 x $\frac{100}{100}$ $ 1,200,000

Owners' equity:
   Capital: $5,000,000 x $\frac{100}{40}$ 12,500,000

   Retained earnings   2,300,000

                                                                                                          $16,000,000

This balance sheet is then rolled forward to dollars of general purchasing power at December 31, 19x5:

Monetary assets: $2,000,000 x $\frac{125}{100}$ $ 2,500,000

Plant and equipment: $20,000,000 x $\frac{125}{100}$ 25,000,000

Accumulated depreciation: $6,000,000 x $\frac{125}{100}$ (7,500,000)

                                                                                                          $20,000,000

Monetary liabilities: $1,200,000 x $\frac{125}{100}$ $ 1,500,000

Owners' equity:
   Capital: $12,500,000 x $\frac{125}{100}$ 15,625,000

   Retained earnings   2,875,000

                                                                                                          $20,000,000

You will recall that the revenue and other expenses appear as of the end of 19x5 when the index is 125.

Revenue: $8,000,000 x $\frac{125}{125}$ $ 8,000,000

Expenses:
   Depreciation: $1,000,000 x $\frac{125}{50}$ (2,500,000)

   Other: $5,000,000 x $\frac{125}{125}$ (5,000,000)

                                        500,000

Loss of general purchasing from holding
   monetary assets in excess of monetary
   liabilities:
     $\left[(\$2,000,000 - \$1,200,000) \times \frac{125}{100}\right]$ minus

     ($2,000,000 - $1,200,000)   200,000*

Net income $ 300,000

*The $200,000 loss arises because a net of $800,000 of monetary assets
($2,000,000 of monetary assets less $1,200,000 of monetary liabilities)
was held for the entire year while the general price index rose from 100
to 125. This means that to buy in *general* goods what would have cost
$800,000 on December 31, 19x4, would cost $1,000,000 as of December 31,
19x5. Since the company has only $800,000 at December 31, 19x5, it is
$200,000 short. The company has lost $200,000 by holding monetary assets
which are fixed in dollars and cannot rise with inflation. To avoid the
$200,000 loss, the company would have to invest in non-monetary items.
But this sacrifices liquidity (see Chapter 14) of the company and may
risk bankruptcy.

We can prove the $300,000 net income figure by reconciling to the difference
in retained earnings:

Balance, December 31, 19x5 $ 3,175,000
Less: Balance, December 31, 19x4   2,875,000
                                       300,000
Dividends   NIL
Net income $ 300,000

Observe that the $200,000 general purchasing power loss arises *during*
19x5 but is measured in dollars of general purchasing power *as of*
December 31, 19x5. The loss of $200,000 is measured in index 125. If it
were measured in index 100, the loss would be 100/125 x $200,000 =
$160,000. This point should be kept in mind as we do case B.

Case B

Since the revenue ($8,000,000) and other expense ($5,000,000) transactions
occur at mid year, and the net $3,000,000 is "invested" in net monetary
assets, a further loss of general purchasing power occurs between mid year
and year end. Neither the opening nor the closing balance sheet change;

only the income statement transactions must be restated from their date of
of occurrence to dollars of general purchasing power as of December 31,
19x5.

Revenue: $8,000,000 x $\frac{125}{112.5}$ $\underline{\$\ 8,888,888}$

Expenses:

Depreciation: $1,000,000 x $\frac{125}{50}$ (2,500,000)

Other: $5,000,000 x $\frac{125}{112.5}$ $\underline{(5,555,555)}$

$\underline{(8,055,555)}$

833,333

Loss of general purchasing power $\underline{533,333*}$

Income $\underline{\$\qquad 300,000}$

*Let us calculate the $533,333 in two ways:

1. We already know from Case A that $800,000 ($2,000,000 − $1,200,000) of
    net monetary assets were held all year and we incurred a loss of
    $200,000. The remaining $333,333 of the loss arises because of the
    mid year transaction which resulted in $3,000,000 ($8,000,000 −
    $5,000,000) of monetary assets being idle, while the general price
    index rose from 112.5 to 125:

$3,000,000 x $\frac{125}{112.5}$ $3,333,333

Less actually on hand $\underline{3,000,000}$ $3,333,33

Add loss on $800,000 $\underline{\qquad 200,000}$

$\underline{\$533,333}$

2. We can also reconstruct the monetary asset and monetary liability
    positions for 19x5.

Monetary Assets Less Monetary Liabilities		
December 31, 19x4	2,000,000	1,200,000
	800,000	
Mid year 19x5	+8,000,000	−5,000,000
	3,800,000	
December 31, 19x5	3,800,000	

The account shows that we held $800,000 net during a general price
index rise from 100 to 112.5 and held $3,800,000 when the index rose
from 112.5 to 125.

a. Held from mid year to year end:

$$\$(3,800,000 \times \frac{125}{112.5}) - \$3,800,000 \qquad\qquad \$422,222$$

b. Held from beginning of year to year end:

$$\$(800,000 \times \frac{112.5}{100}) - \$800,000 = \$100,000$$

The $100,000 would have to be restated from index

112.5 to 125:   111,111

$$\$100,000 \times \frac{125}{112.5} \qquad\qquad\qquad \underline{\$533,333}$$

Observe in part b. that two steps are required: first, to calculate
the loss; and second, to restate the loss to dollars of general purchasing
power at December 31, 19x5. A short cut is not possible!

CURRENT VALUE ACCOUNTING

The term "current value accounting" is a somewhat meaningless description
used to encompass other than historic cost and GPL. As the textbook notes
in several places (page 717 for example) we have to define both our net
asset (asset less liability) valuation bases and our capital maintenance
measurement. Then we can compute annual and lifetime income. The definitions of capital maintenance lead us into Question 10-10 on page 740 of
the textbook.

TEXTBOOK *16-10: A SOLUTION (30-50 minutes)

Capital can be defined and measured in several ways. In general terms,
capital refers to the total investment contributed by the owners (common
and preferred shareholders) plus "donated" surplus and retained earnings.
Income is the "excess" of net asset values at the end of a period over
the opening capital balance, plus or minus changes in capital during the
period (dividends for example, are deductions from capital).

There are many measures of capital, some of which are:

1. Original money investment - The original money investment concept of
    capital is widely used in Canada, especially in external reports.
    "Capital" simply represents all contributions by shareholders (pre-
    ferred and common) plus surplus and retained earnings. "Income"
    (in theory) is therefore the excess of net assets at the end of the
    period over opening capital, including any further contributions,
    less dividends.

2. Original money investment restated for fluctuations in the exchange
   value of the dollar (price level restatement) - this alternative
   involves applying a price index to restate the capital. "Capital"
   thus becomes historic dollars plus or minus overall price changes in
   the economy since the dates of original investment. "Income," being
   the excess of net asset valuations over capital, would delete any
   effects of general inflation (or deflation).

3. Operating capacity measures - emphasis in this family of measures
   is placed on a restatement of all long-term capital, by means of many
   restatements of the specific net assets held by the organization.
   Operating capacity thus represents whatever the organization actually
   possesses from moment to moment. Income under the operating capacity
   concepts of capital is simply the excess received (in the selling
   market) over the current (buying market) price for the item.

The best way to demonstrate the impact which the capital maintenance concept selected has on income is by an example. Suppose a house is bought
at the beginning of the year for $100,000 contributed by an individual,
and sold at the end of the year for $150,000, and during the year the rate
of inflation was 20%. What is the income? It depends on the capital
concept used.

1. Original money investment:

Selling price	$150,000
Original investment	100,000
Income	$ 50,000

In a venture created for a specific purpose and of a limited short
life, this definition of capital makes sense. No additional purchases
of homes is contemplated, no continuity of operations is planned, and
therefore the $50,000 is distributable to the participants of the
joint venture. In this case, original money capital is a reasonable
capital maintenance concept.

2. Restated original money investment:

Selling price	$150,000	
Original investment	120,000	(100,000 x 120%)
Income	$ 30,000	

In periods of inflation the individual may be interested in maintaining
his purchasing power (i.e., ability to buy a basket of goods). Presumably consumption was deferred in favour of buying a new house. Is the
individual "better off"? It depends on his view of what "better off"
implies. If it is his command over a general basket of goods, then
he is $30,000 better off. In companies with continuing operations,
shareholders may wish to assess changes in their purchasing power to
evaluate whether to hold or sell their ownership interest in the
company.

3. Operating capacity measures:

Selling price	$150,000	
Operating capacity capital	(150,000)	(assumes that selling price reflects replacement cost of the house at the end of the
Income	$ NIL	year)

If the individual intends to replace the house sold with a new house, is he "better off"? Assuming that the cost to replace the house is $150,000, then he is no "better off." In this situation capital is defined as the house. For the individual to improve his situation, he would have had to have received more than the cost to replace the house. This concept of capital maintenance is sensible when users of financial statements take a long-term perspective and wish to predict distributable cash flows, assuming the company intends to continue operations indefinitely. In the examples above, since the house must be replaced, there are no distributable profits.

NEW PROBLEM 2 (45-70 minutes)

1. Prepare a balance sheet at December 31, 19x2, and an income statement for 19x2 from the following information:

January 2, 19x1: The company was formed with $100,000 which was credited to common shares. 5,000 tons of steel were purchased for $20 per ton cash.

December 31, 19x1: 3,000 tons were sold for $32 per ton. 4,000 tons of steel of the same quality as the previous purchase were acquired for $23 per ton.

December 31, 19x2: 4,000 tons of steel were sold for $35 per ton. Replacement cost on this date is $28 per ton.

The general price index was:

January 2, 19x1   50
December 31, 19x1   55
December 31, 19x2   66

Prepare your financial statements on the following bases:

	Net Asset Valuation Basis	Capital Maintenance Basis
a.	General price-level restatement of historic cost	General price-level restatement of historic cost

b.   Replacement cost   General price-level
                                        restatement of
                                        historic cost

c.   Replacement cost   Operating or physical
                                        capacity (defined as
                                        5,000 tons)

Assume FIFO cost flows.

2. Explain the circumstances where each of a., b., and c. in 1. would be
a sensible application.

A *Solution*

1. a. GPL.

Although the question asks for 19x2 only, let us prepare 19x1 in order
to gain some experience.

19x1:	Revenue: 3,000 tons at $32		$ 96,000
	Cost of goods sold:		
	3,000 tons x ($20 plus 10%)		66,000
	"Income"		$ 30,000

Balance sheet:

Cash: ($96,000 – $92,000 purchase)			$ 4,000
Inventory:			
2,000 tons at ($20 plus 10%)		$44,000	
4,000 tons at $23		92,000	136,000
			$140,000
Common shares			$100,000
Capital maintenance adjustment			
10% x $100,000			10,000
Retained earnings			30,000
			$140,000

19x2:	Revenue: 4,000 at $35		$140,000
	Cost of goods sold:		
	2,000 tons at (($20 plus 10%) plus 20%)		52,800
	2,000 tons at ($23 plus 20%)		55,200
			108,000
	Gross profit		31,000
	Loss of general purchasing power:		
	($4,000 x 120%) – $4,000		800
	"Income"		$ 31,200

- 199 -

Balance Sheet:

Cash: ($4,000 – $140,000)	$144,000
Inventory: 2,000 tons at ($23 plus 20%)	55,200
	$199,200
Capital	$100,000
Capital maintenance adjustment:	
Opening balance $10,000 times 20% increase in GPL; plus 20% times $100,000 capital	32,000
Retained earnings:	
Opening balance $30,000 times 20% increase in GPL; plus $31,200	67,200
	$199,200

b. Replacement cost for inventory; GPL capital maintenance:

19x1:			
Revenue			$ 96,000
Cost of goods sold: 3,000 at $23			69,000
Gross profit			27,000
Holding gain: 5,000 tons at ($23–$20)		$15,000	
Less capital maintenance adjustment: $100,000 at 10%		10,000	5,000
"Income"			$ 32,000

Balance Sheet:

Cash	$ 4,000
Inventory: 6,000 at $23	138,000
	$142,000
Capital	$100,000
Capital maintenance adjustment:	
10% x $100,000	10,000
Retained earnings	32,000
	$142,000

19x2:			
Revenue			$140,000
Cost of goods sold: 4,000 at $28			112,000
Gross profit			18,000
Holding gain: 6,000 at ($28–$23)		$30,000	
Less capital maintenance adjustment: 20% of capital and capital maintenance adjustment		$22,000	8,000
"Income"			$ 36,000

Balance Sheet:

Cash	$144,000
Inventory: 2,000 at $28	56,000
	$200,000

Capital	$100,000
Capital maintenance adjustment: opening balance $10,000 plus $22,000 added this year	32,000*
Retained earnings: $32,000 from last year plus $36,000	68,000*
	$200,000

*Capital has been defined to exclude retained earnings. If retained earnings is part of the capital to be maintained, retained earnings would be $6,000 ($30,000 opening retained earnings at 20% GPL) lower capital maintenance would be $6,000 higher. "Income" in 19x2 would also be $6,000 lower because the capital maintenance charge would be $28,000 instead of $22,000.

c. Replacement cost and physical capacity capital maintenance:

19x1:

Revenue		$ 96,000
Cost of goods sold		69,000
Gross profit		27,000
Holding gain: 5,000 at ($23–$20)	$15,000	
Less capital maintenance on 5,000 tons at ($23–$20)	15,000	0
"Income"		$ 27,000

Balance Sheet:

Cash	$ 4,000
Inventory: 6,000 at $23	138,000
	$142,000

Capital	$100,000
Capital maintenance adjustment	15,000
Retained earnings	27,000
	$142,000

19x2:

Revenue		$140,000
Cost of goods sold: 4,000 at $28		112,000
Gross profit		28,000
Holding gain: 6,000 at ($28–$23)	$30,000	
Less capital maintenance on 5,000 tons at ($28–$23)	25,000	5,000
"Income"		$ 33,000

Balance sheet:

Cash	$144,000
Inventory: 2,000 at $28	56,000
	$200,000

Capital	$100,000
Capital maintenance adjustment: opening balance $15,000 plus $25,000 from this year	40,000
Retained earnings: $27,000 opening balance plus $33,000 this year	60,000
	$200,000

2. The benefits of a. (GPL) are not clear. Some *new* information is provided by the loss of purchasing power in 19x2 but the balance sheets
display questionable figures. See pages 729-730 of the textbook. We
have to consider who wants to use the information and for what purpose.
GPL would be adequate for stewardship purposes if no historic cost
financial statements existed. But GPL is not currently acceptable for
income tax purposes. It is not particularly useful for the other
objectives of accounting. See pages 182 to 188 of the textbook.

Methods b. and c. use replacement cost valuations for inventory. Hence,
if we wish to predict, we know the expected cash outflow to replace the
items. In conjunction with a capital maintenance measure, we might be
able to form an assessment of overall management performance. GPL
capital maintenance is easier to implement than is operating capacity
defined as 5,000 tons of inventory. The conceptual aspect of capital
maintenance is discussed in *16-10, which we responded to earlier.

The key to answering this type of question is to make sure that you
respond to *both* the net asset value measure (in this case replacement
cost for inventory) and to the capital maintenance measure. For
instance, although b. and c. use replacement cost for net asset values,
company c. may have chosen operating capacity to stress that it does
not make a "profit" unless it can replace its inventory. That is, it
is stressing continuity forever.